P9-DHL-837

DOVER · THRIFT · EDITIONS

Great Poems by American Women

An Anthology

Edited by

SUSAN L. RATTINER

DOVER PUBLICATIONS, INC.
Mineola, New York

DOVER THRIFT EDITIONS

GENERAL EDITOR: PAUL NEGRI
EDITOR OF THIS VOLUME: SUSAN L. RATTINER

ACKNOWLEDGMENTS: see page xv.

Copyright

Copyright © 1998 by Dover Publications, Inc.
All rights reserved under Pan American and International Copyright Conventions.

Bibliographical Note

Great Poems by American Women is a new anthology, first published by Dover Publications, Inc., in 1998.

Library of Congress Cataloging-in-Publication Data

Great poems by American women : an anthology / edited by Susan L. Rattiner.
     p.   cm. — (Dover thrift editions)
  Includes index.
  ISBN 0-486-40164-2 (pbk.)
  1. American poetry—Women authors.   I. Rattiner, Susan L.   II. Series.
PS589.G68   1998
811.008'09287—dc21

98-4391
CIP

Manufactured in the United States of America
Dover Publications, Inc., 31 East 2nd Street, Mineola, N.Y. 11501

Note

From the sentimentality of Anne Bradstreet to the raw emotion of Sylvia Plath, this anthology represents the great diversity in style and substance of American women's poetry from colonial times to the twentieth century. In the seventeenth and eighteenth centuries, women poets primarily wrote for their own pleasure and never expected to have their work published. Anne Bradstreet was the first colonial woman poet in America. Bradstreet's most amazing accomplishment as a poet was the publication of her verse in 1650. Her poems, focusing on traditional female roles, traversed such topics as motherhood, marriage, and domestic life. Unlike most of the other early poets in this anthology, Bradstreet was encouraged to write by her husband.

Acquiescing to the demands and pressures of their spouses and other family members, many women poets were forced to abandon their writing. Prevailing male attitudes hindered the female poet's originality and creativity. "It is less easy to be assured of the genuineness of literary ability in women than in men": this is the opening sentence to Rufus W. Griswold's preface to *The Female Poets of America* in 1849. Even the anthologist himself, hailed for bringing these women poets to the public, subscribes to the gender stereotype. Ironically, Griswold's anthology was one of the first devoted exclusively to women's verse and yet fostered the male-centered values of nineteenth-century American culture.

Over the next several decades, subsequent anthologies of women's poetry appeared, including Caroline May's *The American Female Poets*, and several others. However, only a select few poets, such as Emily Dickinson, Emma Lazarus, and Edna St. Vincent Millay, left a lasting impression. A large number of minor poets have no name recognition today since they were omitted from later collections. Most women poets in the nineteenth century contributed their verse to newspapers, magazines, and journals wishing to increase female readership. Poets submitted what became known as *potboilers*, seemingly inferior works that were turned out for quick profit. These poets were usually widows with children to raise, and their writing became their livelihood. The transient nature of these periodicals ensured that these women writers did not achieve an enduring fame. In many cases, the poems became famous, and the poet's name fell by the wayside. "America the Beautiful," written by Katharine Lee Bates in 1893 after climbing Pike's Peak, was set to music by Horatio Parker. Very few people know that this was written by a woman, and even fewer can recall her name.

A large percentage of the poets featured here were born in New England, where there were greater educational opportunities. In the eighteenth century, Mercy Otis Warren gleaned her education from her brother's tutor, later writing a three-volume history of the American Revolution based on her diary. A mother of five children, Warren also wrote political plays in addition to poetry. Phillis Wheatley, brought to America on a slave ship, was the first African-American woman poet. She was educated with her master's children and urged to pursue publication. Another female pioneer was Emma Hart Willard, who started the first secondary school for women. She taught women all the subjects traditionally considered to be "male," including history, geography, trigonometry, and algebra. Willard was responsible for training hundreds of women as teachers.

Spanning more than three centuries of women's verse, this anthology, containing 209 poems, hopes to rescue many long-forgotten poets from obscurity. Since many of these poets are unfamiliar to readers today, a brief biographical note precedes each selection. This volume represents just a sampling of American women poets—many were omitted for reasons of space. The dearth of information about some of these women poets is astounding; poems may have been lost over time, discarded in old journals, or destroyed. Anonymous publications, multiple pseudonyms, and surname changes with marriages and remarriages all combine to make gathering biographical data a difficult task. As a result, information about some of these women is sketchy at best. The seventy-four poets in this collection are arranged chronologically, providing the reader with a fine introduction to America's women poets.

Contents

Acknowledgments

Louise Bogan: "Medusa" and "Women" from *The Blue Estuaries* by Louise Bogan. Copyright © 1968 by Louise Bogan. Copyright renewed © 1996 by Ruth Limmer. Reprinted by permission of Farrar, Straus & Giroux, Inc.

Gwendolyn Brooks: "Jessie Mitchell's Mother" by Gwendolyn Brooks. Copyright © 1991, from *Blacks*, published by Third World Press, Chicago, 1991. Reprinted with the permission of Gwendolyn Brooks.

Hilda Doolittle: "Helen" by H.D., from *Collected Poems, 1912–1944*. Copyright © 1982 by The Estate of Hilda Doolittle. Reprinted by permission of New Directions Publishing Corp.

Edna St. Vincent Millay: "I, being born a woman and distressed," "Euclid alone has looked on Beauty bare," and "What lips my lips have kissed, and where, and why" by Edna St. Vincent Millay. From *Collected Poems*, HarperCollins. Copyright 1923, 1951 by Edna St. Vincent Millay and Norma Millay Ellis. All rights reserved. Reprinted by permission of Elizabeth Barnett, literary executor.

Marianne Moore: "Poetry" by Marianne Moore reprinted with the permission of Simon & Schuster from *The Collected Poems of Marianne Moore*. Copyright 1935 by Marianne Moore; copyright renewed © 1963 by Marianne Moore and T.S. Eliot.

Dorothy Parker: "One Perfect Rose" and "Unfortunate Coincidence" by Dorothy Parker, copyright 1926, renewed © 1954 by Dorothy Parker, from *The Portable Dorothy Parker* by Dorothy Parker, Introduction by Brendan Gill. Used by permission of Viking Penguin, a division of Penguin Putnam, Inc.

Sylvia Plath: "Daddy" and "Lady Lazarus" from *Ariel* by Sylvia Plath. Copyright © 1963 by Ted Hughes. Copyright renewed. Reprinted by permission of HarperCollins Publishers, Inc.

Sara Teasdale: "Appraisal" and "The Solitary" by Sara Teasdale reprinted with the permission of Simon & Schuster from *The Collected Poems of Sara Teasdale*. Copyright © 1926 by Macmillan Publishing Company, renewed 1954 by Mamie T. Wheless.

Elinor Wylie: "Let No Charitable Hope" from *Collected Poems* by Elinor Wylie. Copyright 1932 by Alfred A. Knopf, Inc. and renewed 1960 by Edwina C. Rubenstein. Reprinted by permission of the publisher.

ANNE BRADSTREET (1612?–1672)

The first colonial woman poet, Anne Bradstreet came to Massachusetts Bay in 1630. Her poetry was first published in London in 1650 under the title *The Tenth Muse Lately Sprung Up in America* and later in a posthumous edition. Both her father and her husband became governors of the colony. Much of her poetry reflects themes in her personal life—her relationship with her husband and her eight children. Bradstreet's poems also contain her religious outlook and perceptions.

The Prologue

To sing of Wars, of Captains, and of Kings,
Of Cities founded, Common-wealths begun,
For my mean pen are too superiour things,
Or how they all or each their dates have run:
Let Poets and Historians set these forth;
My obscure Lines shall not so dim their worth.

But when my wondring eyes and envious heart
Great *Bartas* sugar'd lines do but read o're,
Fool, I do grudg the Muses did not part
'Twixt him and me that overfluent store;
A *Bartas* can do what a *Bartas* will,
But simple I according to my skill.

From school-boyes tongue no rhet'rick we expect,
Nor yet a sweet Consort from broken strings,
Nor perfect beauty where's a main defect:
My foolish, broken, blemish'd Muse so sings;
And this to mend, alas, no Art is able,
'Cause nature made it so irreparable.

Nor can I, like that fluent sweet-tongu'd Greek
Who lisp'd at first, in future times speak plain;
By Art he gladly found what he did seek,

A full requital of his striving pain:
Art can do much; but this maxime's most sure,
A weak or wounded brain admits no cure.

I am obnoxious to each carping tongue
Who says my hand a needle better fits;
A Poets pen all scorn I should thus wrong,
For such despite they cast on Female wits:
If what I do prove well it won't advance;
They'l say it's stoln, or else it was by chance.

But sure the antique Greeks were far more mild,
Else of our Sexe why feigned they those Nine,
And poesy made *Calliope*'s own Child?
So 'mongst the rest they placed the Arts Divine.
But this weak knot they will full soon untie:
The Greeks did nought but play the fools & lye.

Let Greeks be Greeks, and women what they are,
Men have precedency and still excell:
It is but vain unjustly to wage warre;
Men can do best, and women know it well:
Preheminence in all and each is yours;
Yet grant some small acknowledgement of ours.

And oh ye high flown quills that soar the Skies,
And ever with your prey still catch your praise,
If e're you daigne these lowly lines your eyes,
Give Thyme or Parsley wreath, I ask no bayes:
This mean and unrefined ure of mine,
Will make your glistring gold but more to shine.

The Author to Her Book

Thou ill-formed offspring of my feeble brain,
Who after birth didst by my side remain,
Till snatched from thence by friends, less wise than true,
Who thee abroad, exposed to public view,
Made thee in rags, halting to th' press to trudge,
Where errors were not lessened (all may judge).
At thy return my blushing was not small,
My rambling brat (in print) should mother call,
I cast thee by as one unfit for light,

Thy visage was so irksome in my sight;
Yet being mine own, at length affection would
Thy blemishes amend, if so I could:
I washed thy face, but more defects I saw,
And rubbing off a spot still made a flaw.
I stretched thy joints to make thee even feet,
Yet still thou run's more hobbling than is meet;
In better dress to trim thee was my mind,
But nought save homespun cloth i' th' house I find.
In this array 'mongst vulgars may'st thou roam.
In critic's hands beware thou dost not come,
And take thy way where yet thou art not known;
And for thy mother, she alas is poor,
Which caused her thus to send thee out of door.

To My Dear and Loving Husband

If ever two were one, then surely we.
If ever man were loved by wife, then thee;
If ever wife was happy in a man,
Compare with me, ye women, if you can.
I prize thy love more than whole mines of gold
Or all the riches that the East doth hold.
My love is such that rivers cannot quench,
Nor ought but love from thee, give recompense.
Thy love is such I can no way repay,
The heavens reward thee manifold, I pray.
Then while we live, in love let's so persevere
That when we live no more, we may live ever.

Before the Birth of One of Her Children

All things within this fading world hath end,
Adversity doth still our joys attend;
No ties so strong, no friends so dear and sweet,
But with death's parting blow is sure to meet.
The sentence past is most irrevocable,
A common thing, yet oh, inevitable.
How soon, my Dear, death may my steps attend,
How soon't may be thy lot to lose thy friend,
We both are ignorant, yet love bids me
These farewell lines to recommend to thee,

That when that knot's untied that made us one,
I may seem thine, who in effect am none.
And if I see not half my days that's due,
What nature would, God grant to yours and you;
The many faults that well you know I have
Let be interred in my oblivious grave;
If any worth or virtue were in me,
Let that live freshly in thy memory
And when thou feel'st no grief, as I no harms,
Yet love thy dead, who long lay in thine arms.
And when thy loss shall be repaid with gains
Look to my little babes, my dear remains.
And if thou love thyself, or loved'st me,
These O protect from step-dame's injury.
And if chance to thine eyes shall bring this verse,
With some sad sighs honour my absent hearse;
And kiss this paper for thy love's dear sake,
Who with salt tears this last farewell did take.

MERCY OTIS WARREN (1728–1814)

Historian and poet Mercy Otis Warren, born in Barnstable, Massachusetts, had no formal schooling. Her brother, James Otis, who opposed the Stamp Act of 1765, and her husband, political leader James Warren, kept her in the forefront of politics. She wrote several plays, including the satires *The Adulateur* (1773) and *The Group* (1775). One of the earliest American feminists, Warren corresponded with Abigail Adams, arguing that women were not given the same educational opportunities as men. Warren published *Poems, Dramatic and Miscellaneous* (1790) and the three-volume *A History of the Rise, Progress, and Termination of the American Revolution* (1805). She also corresponded with important political figures of the time such as John Adams, Samuel Adams, Thomas Jefferson, and Elbridge Gerry.

To an Amiable Friend Mourning the Death of an Excellent Father

Let deep dejection hide her pallid face,
And from thy breast each painful image rase;
Forbid thy lip to utter one complaint,
But view the glories of the rising saint,
Ripe for a crown, and waiting the reward
Of watching long the vineyard of the Lord.

The generous purpose of his zealous heart,
Truth to enforce, and knowledge to impart,
Insures his welcome on the unknown shore,
Where choirs of saints, and angel forms adore.
A seraph met him on the trackless way,
And strung his harp to join the heavenly lay.

Complain no more of Death's extensive power,
Whose sceptre wafts us to some blissful shore;
Where the rough billows that roll o'er the head,
That shake the frame, and fill the mind with dread,
Are hush'd in silence, and the soul serene
Looks back delighted on the closing scene.

Happy, thrice happy, that exalted mind,
Who, leaving earth and all its cares behind,
Has not a wish to ruffle or control
The equal temper of his tranquil soul,
Who, on a retrospect, is safe within;

No private passion, nor a darling sin,
Can check his hope, when death's insatiate pow'r,
Stands hovering on the last decisive hour.

Then weep no more, my friend, but all resigned,
Submit thy will to the Eternal Mind,
Who watches o'er the movements of the just,
And will again reanimate the dust!
Thy sire commands, suppress the rising sigh,
He wipes the tear from thy too filial eye,
And bids thee contemplate a soul set free,
Just safe escaped from life's tempestuous sea.

ANN ELIZA BLEECKER (1752–1783)

Ann Eliza Bleecker of New York City was born into one of the wealthiest aristo-
cratic families in the colony. Her poems, including some about the Revolutionary
War, were collected and published posthumously in 1793. Bleecker also wrote a
novel in letter form, *The History of Maria Kittle*, which was the story of an
American woman captured by Indians during the French and Indian War.
Bleecker married at seventeen and settled in Tomhanick, New York, a village
where her husband owned property. When Bleecker moved to Albany in 1777, she
lost her youngest child to illness, and her husband was taken prisoner for several
days in 1781. In 1783, and with failing health, Bleecker and her husband returned
to Tomhanick, where she died at the age of thirty-one.

Return to Tomhanick

Hail, happy shades! though clad with heavy snows,
At sight of you with joy my bosom glows;
Ye arching pines, that bow with every breeze,
Ye poplars, elms, all hail! my well-known trees!
And now my peaceful mansion strikes my eye,
And now the tinkling rivulet I spy;
My little garden, Flora, hast thou kept,
And watch'd my pinks and lilies, while I wept?
Or has the grubbing swine, by furies led,
The enclosure broke, and on my flowrets fed?
Ah me! that spot with blooms so lately grac'd,
With storms and driving snows, is now defaced;
Sharp icicles from every bush depend,
And frosts all dazzling o'er the beds extend:
Yet soon fair spring shall give another scene,
And yellow cowslips gild the level green;
My little orchard sprouting at each bough,
Fragrant with clustering blossoms deep shall glow:
Ah! then 't is sweet the tufted grass to tread,
But sweeter slumbering is the balmy shade;
The rapid humming-bird, with ruby breast,
Seeks the parterre with early blue-bells drest,
Drinks deep the honeysuckle dew, or drives
The labouring bee to her domestic hives:

Then shines the lupine bright with morning gems,
And sleepy poppies nod upon their stems,
The humble violet, and the dulcet rose,
The stately lily then, and tulip blows.

   Farewell, my Plutarch! farewell, pen and muse!
Nature exults—shall I her call refuse?
Apollo fervid glitters in my face,
And threatens with his beam each feeble grace:
Yet still around the lovely plants I toil,
And draw obnoxious herbage from the soil;
Or with the lime-twigs little birds surprise;
Or angle for the trout of many dyes.

   But when the vernal breezes pass away,
And loftier Phoebus darts a fiercer ray,
The spiky corn then rattles all around,
And dashing cascades give a pleasing sound;
Shrill sings the locust with prolonged note,
The cricket chirps familiar in each cot.
The village children, rambling o'er yon hill,
With berries all their painted baskets fill.
They rob the squirrel's little walnut store,
And climb the half-exhausted tree for more;
Or else to fields of maze nocturnal hie,
Where hid, the elusive water-melons lie;
Sportive, they make incisions in the rind,
The riper from the immature to find;
Then load their tender shoulders with the prey,
And laughing, bear the bulky fruit away.

An Evening Prospect

Come, my Susan, quit your chamber,
   Greet the opening bloom of May,
Let us up yon hillock clamber,
   And around the scene survey.

See the sun is now descending,
   And projects his shadows far,
And the bee her course is bending
   Homeward through the humid air.

Mark the lizard just before us,
    Singing her unvaried strain,
While the frog abrupt in chorus
    Deepens through the marshy plain.

From yon grove the woodcock rises,
    Mark her progress by her notes,
High in air her wing she poises,
    Then like lightning down she shoots.

Now the whip-poor-will beginning,
    Clamorous on a pointed rail,
Drowns the more melodious singing
    Of the catbird, thrush, and quail.

Pensive Echo from the mountain
    Still repeats the sylvan sounds;
And the crocus-bordered fountain
    With the splendid fly abounds.

There the honey-suckle blooming,
    Reddens the capricious wave;
Richer sweets, the air perfuming,
    Spicy Ceylon never gave.

Cast your eyes beyond this meadow,
    Painted by a hand divine,
And observe the ample shadow
    Of that solemn ridge of pine.

Here a trickling rill depending,
    Glitters through the artless bower
And the silver dew descending,
    Doubly radiates every flower.

While I speak, the sun is vanish'd,
    All the gilded clouds are fled;
Music from the groves is banish'd,
    Noxious vapours round us spread.

Rural toil is now suspended,
    Sleep invades the peasant's eyes;
Each diurnal task is ended,
    While soft Luna climbs the skies

Queen of rest and meditation!
    Through thy medium, I adore
Him—the Author of creation,
    Infinite and boundless power!

He now fills thy urn with glory,
    Transcript of immortal light;
Lord! my spirit bows before thee,
    Lost in wonder and delight.

PHILLIS WHEATLEY (1753?–1784)

Born in Africa, Phillis Wheatley was brought to America on a slave ship in 1761. Servant for a wealthy Boston tailor and his wife, Wheatley was the first black American woman poet. Educated with the Wheatley's other children, she learned English quickly and mastered Greek and Latin as well. She began writing poetry when she was thirteen, and published her first book, *Poems on Various Subjects, Religious and Moral,* in 1773. After the death of her mistress, Wheatley was freed, and married a free black, John Peters, in 1778. Abolitionists often used Wheatley's poems to promote education for people of all races. *Memoir and Poems of Phillis Wheatley* (1834) and *Letters of Phillis Wheatley, the Negro Slave-Poet of Boston* (1864) were published posthumously.

On Being Brought from Africa to America

'Twas mercy brought me from my pagan land,
Taught my benighted soul to understand
That there's a God, that there's a Savior too:
Once I redemption neither sought nor knew.
Some view our sable race with scornful eye,
"Their color is a diabolic dye."
Remember, Christians, Negroes, black as Cain,
May be refin'd, and join th' angelic train.

To S. M., a Young African Painter, on Seeing His Works

To show the lab'ring bosom's deep intent,
And thought in living characters to paint,
When first thy pencil did those beauties give,
And breathing figures learnt from thee to live,
How did those prospects give my soul delight,
A new creation rushing on my sight?
Still, wond'rous youth! each noble path pursue,
On deathless glories fix thine ardent view:
Still may the painter's and the poet's fire
To aid thy pencil, and thy verse conspire!
And may the charms of each seraphic theme
Conduct thy footsteps to immortal fame!
High to the blissful wonders of the skies
Elate thy soul, and raise thy wishful eyes.
Thrice happy, when exalted to survey
That splendid city, crown'd with endless day,

11

Whose twice six gates on radiant hinges ring:
Celestial *Salem* blooms in endless spring.

    Calm and serene thy moments glide along,
And may the muse inspire each future song!
Still, with the sweets of contemplation bless'd,
May peace with balmy winds your soul invest!
But when these shades of time are chas'd away,
And darkness ends in everlasting day,
On what seraphic pinions shall we move,
And view the landscapes in the realms above?
There shall thy tongue in heav'nly murmurs flow,
And there my muse with heav'nly transport glow:
No more to tell of *Damon's* tender sighs,
Or rising radiance of *Aurora's* eyes,
For nobler themes demand a nobler strain,
And purer language on th' ethereal plain.
Cease, gentle muse! the solemn gloom of night
Now seals the fair creation from my sight.

On Imagination

Thy various works, imperial queen, we see,
How bright their forms! how decked with pomp by thee!
The wond'rous acts in beauteous order stand,
And all attest how potent is thine hand.

    From *Helicon's* refulgent heights attend,
Ye sacred choir, and my attempts befriend:
To tell her glories with a faithful tongue,
Ye blooming graces, triumph in my song.

    Now here, now there, the roving *Fancy* flies
Till some loved object strikes her wand'ring eyes,
Whose silken fetters all the senses bind,
And soft captivity involves the mind.

    Imagination! who can sing thy force?
Or who describe the swiftness of thy course?
Soaring through air to find the bright abode,
Th'empyreal palace of the thund'ring God,
We on thy pinions can surpass the wind,
And leave the rolling universe behind:
From star to star the mental optics rove,
Measure the skies, and range the realms above.

There in one view we grasp the mighty whole,
Or with new worlds amaze th'unbounded soul.

Though *Winter* frowns to *Fancy's* raptured eyes
The fields may flourish, and gay scenes arise;
The frozen deeps may break their iron bands,
And bid the waters murmur o'er the sands.
Fair *Flora* may resume her fragrant reign,
And with her flow'ry riches deck the plain;
Sylvanus may diffuse his honours round,
And all the forest may with leaves be crowned:
Show'rs may descend, and dews their gems disclose,
And nectar sparkle on the blooming rose.

Such is thy pow'r, nor are thine orders vain,
O thou the leader of the mental train:
In full perfection all thy works are wrought,
And thine the sceptre o'er the realms of thought.
Before thy throne the subject-passions bow,
Of subject passions sov'reign ruler Thou,
At thy command joy rushes on the heart,
And through the glowing veins the spirits dart.

Fancy might now her silken pinions try
To rise from earth, and sweep th' expanse on high;
From *Tithon's* bed now might *Aurora* rise,
Her cheeks all glowing with celestial dyes,
While a pure stream of light o'erflows the skies.
The monarch of the day I might behold
And all the mountains tipt with radiant gold,
But I reluctant leave the pleasing views,
Which *Fancy* dresses to delight the *Muse*;
Winter austere forbids me to aspire,
And northern tempests damp the rising fire;
They chill the tides of *Fancy's* flowing sea,
Cease then, my song, cease the unequal lay.

On the Death of the Rev. Mr. George Whitefield—1770

Hail, happy saint! on thine immortal throne,
Possessed of glory, life, and bliss unknown:
We hear no more the music of thy tongue;
Thy wonted auditories cease to throng.
Thy sermons in unequalled accents flowed,

And every bosom with devotion glowed;
Thou didst, in strains of eloquence refined,
Inflame the heart, and captivate the mind.
Unhappy, we the setting sun deplore,
So glorious once, but ah! it shines no more.
    Behold the prophet in his towering flight!
He leaves the earth for heaven's unmeasured height,
And worlds unknown receive him from our sight.
There Whitefield wings with rapid course his way,
And sails to Zion through vast seas of day.
Thy prayers, great saint, and thine incessant cries,
Have pierced the bosom of thy native skies.
Thou, moon, hast seen, and all the stars of light,
How he has wrestled with his God by night.
He prayed that grace in every heart might dwell;
He longed to see America excel;
He charged its youth that every grace divine
Should with full lustre in their conduct shine.
That Savior, which his soul did first receive,
The greatest gift that even a God can give,
He freely offered to the numerous throng
That on his lips with list'ning pleasure hung.
    "Take him, ye wretched, for your only good,
Take him, ye starving sinners, for your food;
Ye thirsty, come to this life-giving stream,
Ye preachers, take him for your joyful theme;
Take him, my dear Americans," he said,
"Be your complaints on his kind bosom laid:
Take him, ye Africans, he longs for you;
Impartial Savior, is his title due:
Washed in the fountain of redeeming blood,
You shall be sons, and kings, and priests to God."
    But though arrested by the hand of death,
Whitefield no more exerts his lab'ring breath,
Yet let us view him in the eternal skies,
Let every heart to this bright vision rise;
While the tomb safe retains its sacred trust,
Till life divine reanimates his dust.

An Hymn to the Evening

Soon as the sun forsook the eastern main,
The pealing thunder shook the heav'nly plain:
Majestic grandeur! From the zephyr's wing
Exhales the incense of the blooming spring.
Soft purl the streams; the birds renew their notes,
And through the air their mingled music floats.
Through all the heav'ns what beauteous dies are spread!
But the west glories in the deepest red:
So may our breasts with ev'ry virtue glow,
The living temples of our God below.
Fill'd with the praise of him who gives the light
And draws the sable curtains of the night,
Let placid slumbers sooth each weary mind
At morn to wake more heav'nly, more refin'd;
So shall the labours of the day begin
More pure, more guarded from the snares of sin.
Night's leaden sceptre seals my drowsy eyes;
Then cease, my song, till fair Aurora rise.

SARAH WENTWORTH MORTON (1759–1846)

Born in Boston in 1759, Sarah Wentworth Morton began contributing poems to the *Massachusetts Magazine* under the pseudonyms "Constantia" and "Philenia." "Philenia" earned high praise from British poetry critics, who referred to her as the "American Sappho." Her first volume was a long verse narrative entitled *Ouabi: or The Virtues of Nature* (1790). Her verses simultaneously published in numerous periodicals, Morton is considered the leading American woman poet of her time. Her last book, *My Mind and Its Thoughts*, appeared in 1823, and is the only one published under her real name. The poem included here, "The African Chief," is one in which Morton, the wife of the attorney general of Massachusetts, attacks a very timely subject—slavery.

The African Chief

See how the black ship cleaves the main,
    High bounding o'er the dark blue wave,
Remurmuring with the groans of pain,
    Deep freighted with the princely slave!

Did all the gods of Afric sleep,
    Forgetful of their guardian love,
When the white tyrants of the deep,
    Betray'd him in the palmy grove?

A chief of Gambia's golden shore,
    Whose arm the band of warriors led;
Or more—the lord of generous power,
    By whom the foodless poor were fed.

Does not the voice of reason cry,
    "Claim the first right that nature gave,
From the red scourge of bondage fly,
    Nor deign to live a burden'd slave?"

Has not his suffering offspring clung,
    Desponding, round his fetter'd knee;
On his worn shoulder, weeping hung,
    And urged one effort to be free?

His wife by nameless wrongs subdued,
    His bosom's friend to death resign'd;
The flinty path-way drench'd in blood;
    He saw with cold and frenzied mind.

Strong in despair, he sought the plain,
  To heaven was raised his steadfast eye,
Resolved to burst the crushing chain,
  Or 'mid the battle's blast, to die.

First of his race, he led the band,
  Guardless of danger, hurtling round,
Till by his red avenging hand,
  Full many a despot stained the ground.

When erst Messenia's sons oppress'd,
  Flew desperate to the sanguine field,
With iron clothed each injured breast,
  And saw the cruel Spartan yield,

Did not the soul to heaven allied,
  With the proud heart as greatly swell,
As when the Roman Decius died,
  Or when the Grecian victim fell?

Do later deeds quick rapture raise,
  The boon Batavia's William won,
Paoli's time-enduring praise,
  Or the yet greater Washington?

If these exalt thy sacred zeal,
  To hate oppression's mad control,
For bleeding Afric learn to feel,
  Whose chieftain claimed a kindred soul.

Oh! mourn the last disastrous hour,
  Lift the full eye of bootless grief,
While victory treads the sultry shore,
  And tears from hope the captive chief.

While the hard race of pallid hue,
  Unpractised in the power to feel,
Resign him to the murderous crew,
  The horrors of the quivering wheel.

Let sorrow bathe each blushing cheek,
  Bend piteous o'er the tortured slave,
Whose wrongs compassion cannot speak,
  Whose only refuge was the grave.

SUSANNA HASWELL ROWSON (1762–1824)

Susanna Haswell Rowson, the daughter of a naval lieutenant stationed in Massachusetts, was an author, actress, and educator. Her first novel, *Victoria*, was published in 1786, and Rowson married that same year. In 1791, Rowson published *Charlotte, a Tale of Truth*. Reprinted in 1794, the book was very successful in America. Rowson and her husband acted in the Philadelphia theater in Rowson's comic opera, *Slaves in Algiers* (1794) and a musical, *The Volunteers* (1795). After performing in *Americans in England; or Lessons for Daughters* (1797), Rowson retired from the theater. From 1797–1822, Rowson ran a school for women in Boston. She wrote poetry and songs for her students, edited the *Boston Weekly Magazine*, and also wrote several more novels.

America, Commerce, and Freedom

How blest a life a sailor leads,
　　From clime to clime still ranging;
For as the calm the storm succeeds,
　　The scene delights by changing!
When tempests howl along the main,
　　Some object will remind us,
And cheer with hopes to meet again
　　Those friends we've left behind us.
Then, under snug sail, we laugh at the gale,
　　And though landsmen look pale, never heed 'em;
But toss off a glass to a favorite lass,
　　To America, commerce, and freedom!

And when arrived in sight of land,
　　Or safe in port rejoicing,
Our ship we moor, our sails we hand,
　　Whilst out the boat is hoisting.
With eager haste the shore we reach,
　　Our friends delighted greet us;
And, tripping lightly o'er the beach,
　　The pretty lasses meet us.
When the full-flowing bowl has enlivened the soul,
　　To foot it we merrily lead 'em,
And each bonny lass will drink off a glass
　　To America, commerce, and freedom!

Our cargo sold, the chink we share,
　　And gladly we receive it;

18

And if we meet a brother tar
   Who wants, we freely give it.
No freeborn sailor yet had store,
   But cheerfully would lend it;
And when 't is gone, to sea for more—
   We earn it but to spend it.
Then drink round, my boys, 't is the first of our joys
   To relieve the distressed, clothe and feed 'em:
'T is a task which we share with the brave and the fair
   In this land of commerce and freedom!

To Time

Old Time, thou'rt a sluggard; how long dost thou stay;
   Say, where are the wings, with which poets adorn thee?
Sure 'twas some happy being, who ne'er was away
   From the friend he most loved, and who wished to have shorn thee,
First drew thee with pinions; for had he e'er known
   A long separation, so slow dost thou move,
He'd have pictured thee lame, and with fetters bound down;
   So tedious is absence to friendship and love.

I am sure thou'rt a cheat, for I often have wooed thee
   To tarry, when blest with the friend of my heart:
But you vanished with speed, tho' I eager pursued thee,
   Entreating thee not in such haste to depart.
Then, wretch, thou wast deaf, nor wouldst hear my petition,
   But borrowed the wings of a sparrow or dove;
And now, when I wish thee to take thy dismission
   Till those hours shall return, thou refusest to move.

Song

The rose just bursting into bloom,
   Admired where'er 'tis seen,
Dispenses round a rich perfume,
   The garden's pride and queen;
But gathered from its native bed,
   No longer charms the eye;
Its vivid tints are quickly fled,
   'Twill wither, droop and die.

So woman, when by nature drest
    In charms devoid of art,
Can reign sole empress in each breast,
    Can triumph o'er each heart;
Can bid the soul to virtue rise,
    To virtue prompt the brave;
But sinks oppressed, and drooping dies,
    If once she's made a slave.

EMMA HART WILLARD (1787–1870)

Born in Berlin, Connecticut, Emma Hart Willard was a pioneer in women's higher education. In 1814, Willard opened a school for women in Middlebury, Vermont. In 1818, she sent a letter to Governor DeWitt Clinton of New York outlining the advantages of educating women, and asked for state money to help establish schools for girls. Willard, who trained hundreds of teachers, moved her school to Troy, New York, in 1821. The Troy Female Seminary (renamed the Emma Willard School in 1895) was the first school ever to teach science, mathematics, and social studies to girls. Willard taught all subjects herself, and published geography and history textbooks for use in the school, including *History of the United States, or Republic of America* (1828) and *A System of Universal History in Perspective* (1835). Her only book of verse, *The Fulfillment of a Promise* (1831), included her famous poem "Rocked in the Cradle of the Deep."

Rocked in the Cradle of the Deep

Rocked in the cradle of the deep
I lay me down in peace to sleep;
Secure I rest upon the wave,
For thou, O Lord! hast power to save.
I know thou wilt not slight my call,
For Thou dost mark the sparrow's fall;
And calm and peaceful shall I sleep,
Rocked in the cradle of the deep.

When in the dead of night I lie
And gaze upon the trackless sky,
The star-bespangled heavenly scroll,
The boundless waters as they roll,—
I feel thy wondrous power to save
From perils of the stormy wave:
Rocked in the cradle of the deep,
I calmly rest and soundly sleep.

And such the trust that still were mine,
Though stormy winds swept o'er the brine
Or though the tempest's fiery breath
Roused me from sleep to wreck and death
In ocean cave, still safe with Thee
The germ of immortality!
And calm and peaceful shall I sleep,
Rocked in the cradle of the deep.

SARAH JOSEPHA HALE (1788–1879)

A little known fact about Sarah Josepha Hale is that she wrote the classic children's poem "Mary Had a Little Lamb" (1830). Struggling to support five children after her husband's death, Hale turned to writing, signing her early poems with the name "Cornelia." After she published a novel in 1827, Hale was asked to become editor of the *Ladies' Magazine,* where she wrote essays, poems, and criticisms. She supported humanitarian causes and education for women, working for the Boston Ladies' Peace Society and founding the Seaman's Aid Society in 1833. As editor of the women's magazine *Godey's Lady's Book,* Hale helped it achieve great success. She also published the 36-volume *Woman's Record, or Sketches of Distinguished Women,* which contained over 1,000 biographies. Hale retired as editor of *Godey's* at the age of eighty-nine.

The Watcher

The night was dark and fearful,
　　The blast swept wailing by;
A watcher, pale and tearful,
　　Looked forth with anxious eye:
How wistfully she gazes—
　　No gleam of morn is there!
And then her heart upraises
　　Its agony of prayer.

Within that dwelling lonely,
　　Where want and darkness reign,
Her precious child, her only,
　　Lay moaning in his pain;
And death alone can free him—
　　She feels that this must be:
"But oh! for morn to see him
　　Smile once again on me!"

A hundred lights are glancing
　　In yonder mansion fair,
And merry feet are dancing—
　　They heed not morning there:
Oh, young and lovely creatures,
　　One lamp, from out your store,
Would give that poor boy's features
　　To her fond gaze once more!

The morning sun is shining—
  She heedeth not its ray;
Beside her dead reclining,
  That pale, dead mother lay!
A smile her lip was wreathing,
  A smile of hope and love,
As though she still were breathing—
  "There's light for us above!"

LYDIA HUNTLEY SIGOURNEY (1791–1865)

Known as the "sweet singer of Hartford," Lydia Huntley Sigourney opened a school for women in Connecticut when she was only twenty-three years old. *Moral Pieces, in Prose and Verse* (1815) was her first successful volume of poems, launching a prolific publishing career of more than fifty books. In 1819, Sigourney married a local merchant who disapproved of her writing. However, when her husband's business began to fail, Sigourney began publishing her poems anonymously to support her family. Publishing under her own name after 1833, Sigourney's poetry and essays that appeared in periodicals at this time dealt with topics straight out of the newspapers: a death, a horrific fire, the burial of an Indian woman, or a shipwreck, as appears here. She also wrote an epic poem, novels, and an autobiography, *Letters of Life* (1866).

Indian Names

"How can the red men be forgotten, while so many of our states
and territories, bays, lakes and rivers, are indelibly stamped by
names of their giving?"

Ye say they all have passed away,
    That noble race and brave,
That their light canoes have vanished
    From off the crested wave;
That 'mid the forests where they roamed
    There rings no hunter shout,
But their names is on your waters,
    Ye may not wash it out.

'Tis where Ontario's billow
    Like Ocean's surge is curled,
Where strong Niagara's thunders wake
    The echo of the world.
Where red Missouri bringeth
    Rich tribute from the west,
And Rappahannock sweetly sleeps
    On green Virginia's breast.

Ye say their cone-like cabins,
    That clustered o'er the vale,
Have fled away like withered leaves
    Before the autumn gale,
But their memory liveth on your hills,
    Their baptism on your shore,

Your everlasting rivers speak
   Their dialect of yore.

Old Massachusetts wears it,
   Within her lordly crown,
And broad Ohio bears it,
   Amid his young renown;
Connecticut hath wreathed it
   Where her quiet foliage waves,
And bold Kentucky breathed it hoarse
   Through all her ancient caves.

Wachuset hides its lingering voice
   Within his rocky heart,
And Alleghany graves its tone
   Throughout his lofty chart;
Monadnock on his forehead hoar
   Doth seal the sacred trust,
Your mountains build their monument,
   Though ye destroy their dust.

Ye call these red-browed brethren
   The insects of an hour,
Crushed like the noteless worm amid
   The regions of their power;
Ye drive them from their father's lands,
   Ye break of faith the seal,
But can ye from the court of Heaven
   Exclude their last appeal?

Ye see their unresisting tribes,
   With toilsome step and slow,
On through the trackless desert pass,
   A caravan of woe;
Think ye the Eternal's ear is deaf?
   His sleepless vision dim?
Think ye the *soul's blood* may not cry
   From that far land to him?

To the First Slave Ship

First of that train which cursed the wave,
   And from the rifled cabin bore,

Inheritor of wo,—*the slave*
  To bless his palm-tree's shade no more.

Dire engine!—o'er the troubled main
  Borne on in unresisted state,—
Know'st thou within thy dark domain
  The secrets of thy prison'd freight?—

Hear'st thou *their* moans whom hope hath fled?—
  Wild cries, in agonizing starts?—
Know'st thou thy humid sails are spread
  With ceaseless sighs from broken hearts?—

The fetter'd chieftain's burning tear,—
  The parted lover's mute despair,—
The childless mother's pang severe,—
  The orphan's misery, are there.

Ah!—could'st thou from the scroll of fate
  The annal read of future years,
Stripes,—tortures,—unrelenting hate.
  And death-gasps drown'd in slavery's tears.

Down,—down,—beneath the cleaving main
  Thou fain would'st plunge where monsters lie,
Rather than ope the gates of pain
  For time and for Eternity.—

Oh Afric!—what has been thy crime?—
  That thus like Eden's fratricide,
A mark is set upon thy clime,
  And every brother shuns thy side.—

Yet are thy wrongs, thou long-distrest!—
  Thy burdens, by the world unweigh'd,
Safe in that *Unforgetful Breast*
  Where all the sins of earth are laid.—

Poor outcast slave!—Our guilty land
  Should tremble while she drinks thy tears,
Or sees in vengeful silence stand,
  The beacon of thy shorten'd years;—

Should shrink to hear her sons proclaim
  The sacred truth that heaven is just,—

Shrink even at her Judge's name,—
   "Jehovah,—Saviour of the opprest."

The Sun upon thy forehead frown'd,
   But Man more cruel far than he,
Dark fetters on thy spirit bound:—
   Look to the mansions of the free!

Look to that realm where chains unbind,—
   Where the pale tyrant drops his rod,
And where the patient sufferers find
   A friend,—a father in their God.

The Indian's Welcome to the Pilgrim Fathers

Above them spread a stranger sky;
   Around, the sterile plain;
The rock-bound coast rose frowning nigh;
   Beyond,—the wrathful main:
Chill remnants of the wintry snow
   Still choked the encumbered soil,
Yet forth those Pilgrim Fathers go
   To mark their future toil.

'Mid yonder vale their corn must rise
   In summer's ripening pride,
And there the church-spire woo the skies
   Its sister-school beside.
Perchance mid England's velvet green
   Some tender thought reposed,
Though nought upon their stoic mien
   Such soft regret disclosed.

When sudden from the forest wide
   A red-browed chieftain came,
With towering form, and haughty stride,
   And eye like kindling flame:
No wrath he breathed, no conflict sought,
   To no dark ambush drew,
But simply to the Old World brought
   The welcome of the New.

That welcome was a blast and ban
   Upon thy race unborn;

Was there no seer,—thou fated Man!—
    Thy lavish zeal to warn?
Thou in thy fearless faith didst hail
    A weak, invading band,
But who shall heed thy children's wail
    Swept from their native land?

Thou gav'st the riches of thy streams,
    The lordship o'er thy waves,
The region of thine infant dreams
    And of thy father's graves,—
But who to yon proud mansions, piled
    With wealth of earth and sea,
Poor outcast from thy forest wild,
    Say, who shall welcome thee?

Lines

From a bright hearth-stone of our land,
    A beam hath pass'd away,
A smile, whose cheering influence seem'd
    Like morning to the day;
A sacrificing spirit
    With innate goodness fraught,
That ever for another's weal
    Employ'd its fervid thought.

That beam is gather'd back again
    To the Pure Fount of flame,
That smile the Blessed Source hath found,
    From whence its radiance came,—
That spirit hath a genial clime;
    And yet, methinks, 't will bend
Sometimes, amid familiar haunts,
    Beside the mourning friend.

Yet better 't were to pass away,
    Ere evening shadows fell,
To wrap in chillness, and decay,
    What here was loved so well;
And strew unwither'd flowers around,
    When the last footsteps part,
And leave in every nook of home,
    Sweet memories for the heart.

The Bell of the Wreck

Toll!—Toll!—Toll!
  Thou bell by billows swung,
And night and day thy warning lore
  Repeat with mournful tongue:
Toll for the queenly boat,
  Wrecked on yon rocky shore;
Sea-weed is in her palace halls,
  She rides the surge no more.

Toll for the master bold,
  The high-souled and the brave,
Who ruled her like a thing of life
  Amid the crested wave;
Toll for the hardy crew,
  Sons of the storm and blast,
Who long the tyrant Ocean dared—
  It vanquished them at last.

Toll for the man of God,
  Whose hallowed voice of prayer
Rose calm above the gathered groan
  Of that intense despair,—
How precious were those tones
  On the sad verge of life,
Amid the fierce and freezing storm,
  And the mountain-billows' strife!

Toll for the lover lost
  To the gay bridal train—
Bright glows a picture on his breast,
  Beneath the unfathomed main;—
One from her casement bendeth
  Long, o'er the misty sea,—
He cometh not—pale maiden—
  His heart is cold to thee.

Toll for the absent sire,
  Who to his home drew near
To bless that glad expecting group—
  Fond wife, and children dear.
They heap the blazing hearth,
  The festal board is spread,

But a fearful guest is at the gate, —
   Room for the sheeted dead!

Toll for the loved and fair,
   The whelmed beneath the tide,
The broken harps, around whose strings
   The dull sea-monsters glide.
Mother, and nursling sweet
   Reft from the household throng,
There's bitter weeping in the nest
   Where breathed their soul of song.

Toll for the hearts that bleed,
   'Neath misery's furrowed trace,
For the lone, hapless orphan, left
   The last of all his race.
Yea, with thine heaviest knell,
   From surge to echoing shore,
Toll for the living — not the dead
   Whose mortal woes are o'er.

Toll! Toll! — Toll
   O'er breeze and billow free,
And with thy startling voice instruct
   Each rover of the sea;
Tell how o'er proudest joys
   May swift destruction sweep,
And bid him build his hopes on high,
   Lone teacher of the deep.

MARIA GOWEN BROOKS (1794–1845)

Maria Gowen Brooks, also known as "Maria del Occidente," grew up in a prosperous family. After her father's death, Brooks married her much-older widowed brother-in-law when she was only sixteen years old. After falling in love with a young Canadian officer, Brooks began to write poetry, and published *Judith, Esther, and Other Poems* in 1820. When her husband died in 1823, Brooks moved to Cuba with her son and stepsons. While there, she wrote a verse romance, *Zóphiël; or, the Bride of Seven*, which was the first book-length poem written by an American woman. In 1826, Brooks began corresponding with English poet Robert Southey, who admired her works. *Idomen* (1843), an autobiographical story, was published serially in the Boston *Saturday Evening Gazette*. Maria Gowen Brooks died of tropical fever in 1845.

Stanzas

Oh! would I were as firm and cold
As rock that guards some barren isle
And ever bears an aspect bold,
Unmoved though heaven frown or smile,

Heeding alike the dashing wave
That rages 'gainst its beaten breast,
And the soft sea-bird in its cave
By parent bosom gently prest.

But such a rock's frail weed, all white
With the wild ocean-spray would be,
When wandering day-beams lend it light,
A meeter simile for me.

When smiles bedeck the face of heaven
It sparkles back a kindred ray—
But, come one angry blast, 'tis driven
And all its lustre dashed away.

Oh! never was I doomed to know
Thine influence, sweet tranquillity,
But to endure whole months of woe
For every throb of ecstasy.

Would I could meet thee, marble death—
Feel undismayed thy cold embrace,
In thy dark bed resign my breath,
For such the only resting place.

Song

Day, in melting purple dying,
Blossoms, all around me sighing,
Fragrance, from the lilies straying,
Zephyr, with my ringlets playing,
        Ye but waken my distress;
        I am sick of loneliness.

Thou, to whom I love to hearken,
Come, ere night around me darken;
Though thy softness but deceive me,
Say thou'rt true, and I'll believe thee;
        Veil, if ill, thy soul's intent,
        Let me think it innocent!

Save thy toiling, spare thy treasure:
All I ask is friendship's pleasure;
Let the shining ore lie darkling,
Bring no gem in lustre sparkling!
        Gifts and gold are nought to me;
        I would only look on thee!

Tell to thee the highwrought feeling,
Ecstasy but in revealing;
Paint to thee the deep sensation,
Rapture in participation,
        Yet but torture, if compressed
        In a lone, unfriended breast.

Absent still! Ah! come and bless me!
Let these eyes again caress thee;
Once, in caution, I could fly thee:
Now, I nothing could deny thee;
        In a look if death there be,
        Come, and I will gaze on thee!

LYDIA MARIA CHILD (1802–1880)

Born in Medford, Massachusetts, Lydia Maria Child was a pioneer in thought, advocating abolitionism, women's suffrage, and sex education. She and her husband worked together for abolitionism, editing the *National Anti-Slavery Standard* in New York. Child founded a monthly magazine for children and published several best-selling books for women: *The Frugal Housewife* (1829), containing money-saving suggestions for the household; *The Mother's Book* (1831), urging parents to teach their children about sex education; and *A History of the Condition of Women in Various Ages and Nations* (1835). When Child published *An Appeal in Favor of That Class of Americans Called Africans* (1833), she was ostracized from social and literary circles, and the sales of her books declined. Despite all of her social crusading, Child is best remembered for these opening lines from a poem she wrote in 1857: "Over the river, and through the wood,/To grandfather's house we go."

The World I Am Passing Through

Few, in the days of early youth,
Trusted like me in love and truth.
I've learned sad lessons from the years;
But slowly, and with many tears;
For God made me to kindly view
The world that I was passing through.

How little did I once believe
That friendly tones could e'er deceive!
That kindness, and forbearance long,
Might meet ingratitude and wrong!
I could not help but kindly view
The world that I was passing through.

And though I've learned some souls are base,
I would not, therefore, hate the race;
I still would bless my fellow men,
And trust them, though deceived again.
God help me still to kindly view
The world that I am passing through!

Through weary conflicts I have passed,
And struggled into rest at last;
Such rest as when the rack has broke
A joint, or nerve, at every stroke.
The wish survives to kindly view
The world that I am passing through.

From all that fate has brought to me
I strive to learn humility,
And trust in Him who rules above,
Whose universal law is love.
Thus only can I kindly view
The world that I am passing through.

When I approach the setting sun,
And feel my journey nearly done,
May earth be veiled in genial light,
And her last smile to me seem bright!
Help me till then to kindly view
The world that I am passing through!

And all who tempt a trusting heart
From faith and hope to drift apart,—
May they themselves be spared the pain
Of losing power to trust again!
God help us all to kindly view
The world that we are passing through!

The New-England Boy's Song About Thanksgiving Day

Over the river, and through the wood,
    To grandfather's house we go;
        The horse knows the way,
        To carry the sleigh,
    Through the white and drifted snow.

Over the river, and through the wood,
    To grandfather's house away!
        We would not stop
        For doll or top,
    For 't is Thanksgiving day.

Over the river, and through the wood,
    Oh, how the wind does blow!
        It stings the toes,
        And bites the nose,
    As over the ground we go.

Over the river, and through the wood,
    With a clear blue winter sky,
        The dogs do bark,

And children hark,
As we go jingling by.

Over the river, and through the wood,
To have a first-rate play—
Hear the bells ring
Ting a ling ding,
Hurra for Thanksgiving day!

Over the river, and through the wood—
No matter for winds that blow;
Or if we get
The sleigh upset,
Into a bank of snow.

Over the river, and through the wood,
To see little John and Ann;
We will kiss them all,
And play snow-ball,
And stay as long as we can.

Over the river, and through the wood,
Trot fast, my dapple grey!
Spring over the ground,
Like a hunting hound,
For 't is Thanksgiving day!

Over the river, and through the wood,
And straight through the barn-yard gate;
We seem to go
Extremely slow,
It is so hard to wait.

Over the river, and through the wood—
Old Jowler hears our bells;
He shakes his pow,
With a loud bow wow,
And thus the news he tells.

Over the river, and through the wood—
When grandmother sees us come,
She will say, Oh dear,
The children are here,
Bring a pie for every one.

Over the river, and through the wood—
　　Now grandmother's cap I spy!
　　　　Hurra for the fun!
　　　　Is the pudding done?
　　Hurra for the pumpkin pie!

SARAH HELEN WHITMAN (1803–1878)

Sarah Helen Whitman was among the most popular women poets in the mid-nineteenth century. Born in Providence, Rhode Island, Whitman was influenced by the poetry of Byron. She married a Boston editor in 1828 and published her early poems in the *Boston Spectator and Ladies' Album* under the name "Helen." Her work also appeared in Sarah Josepha Hale's *Ladies' Magazine* and in a variety of other periodicals under the name "Egeria." Whitman's husband died in 1833, and she continued to write steadily. In 1848, she published some sonnets to Edgar Allan Poe and received an answer in his poem "To Helen." Whitman and Poe were engaged for a time, but Whitman was advised against the marriage by her mother. Her books include *Hours of Life, and Other Poems* (1853), *Edgar Poe and His Critics* (1860), and *Poems* (1879), collected after her death in 1878. Whitman also served as vice president of the Rhode Island women's suffrage association.

To Edgar Allan Poe

If thy sad heart, pining for human love,
In its earth solitude grew dark with fear,
Lest the high Sun of Heaven itself should prove
Powerless to save from that phantasmal sphere
Wherein thy spirit wandered,—if the flowers
That pressed around thy feet, seemed but to bloom
In lone Gethsemanes, through starless hours,
When all who loved had left thee to thy doom,—
Oh, yet believe that in that hollow vale
Where thy soul lingers, waiting to attain
So much of Heaven's sweet grace as shall avail
To lift its burden of remorseful pain,
My soul shall meet thee, and its Heaven forego
Till God's great love, on both, one hope, one Heaven bestow.

To ——

Vainly my heart had with thy sorceries striven:
It had no refuge from thy love,—no Heaven
But in thy fatal presence;—from afar
It owned thy power and trembled like a star
O'erfraught with light and splendor. Could I deem
How dark a shadow should obscure its beam?—
Could I believe that pain could ever dwell
Where thy bright presence cast its blissful spell?
Thou wert my proud palladium;—could I fear

37

The avenging Destinies when thou wert near?—
Thou wert my Destiny;—thy song, thy fame,
The wild enchantments clustering round thy name,
Were my soul's heritage, its royal dower;
Its glory and its kingdom and its power!

Sonnet V

On our lone pathway bloomed no earthly hopes:
Sorrow and death were near us, as we stood
Where the dim forest, from the upland slopes,
Swept darkly to the sea. The enchanted wood
Thrilled, as by some foreboding terror stirred;
And as the waves broke on the lonely shore,
In their low monotone, methought I heard
A solemn voice that sighed, "Ye meet no more."
There, while the level sunbeams seemed to burn
Through the long aisles of red, autumnal gloom,—
Where stately, storied cenotaphs inurn
Sweet human hopes, too fair on Earth to bloom,—
Was the bud reaped, whose petals pure and cold
Sleep on my heart till Heaven the flower unfold.

The Morning-Glory

When the peach ripens to a rosy bloom,
When purple grapes glow through the leafy gloom
Of trellised vines, bright wonder, thou dost come,
Cool as a star dropt from night's azure dome,
To light the early morning, that doth break
More softly beautiful for thy sweet sake.

Thy fleeting glory to my fancy seems
Like the strange flowers we gather in our dreams;
Hovering so lightly o'er the slender stem,
Wearing so meekly the proud diadem
Of penciled rays, that gave the name you bear
Unblamed amid the flowers, from year to year.
The tawny lily, flecked with jetty studs,
Pard-like, and dropping through long, pendent buds,
Her purple anthers; nor the poppy, bowed
In languid sleep, enfolding in a cloud

Of drowsy odors her too fervid heart,
Pierced by the day-god's barbed and burning dart;
Nor the swart sunflower, her dark brows enrolled
With their broad carcanets of living gold,—
A captive princess, following the car
Of her proud conqueror; nor that sweet star,
The evening primrose, pallid with strange dreams
Born of the wan moon's melancholy beams;
Nor any flower that doth its tendrils twine
Around my memory, hath a charm like thine.
Child of the morning, passionless and fair
As some ethereal creature of the air,
Waiting not for the bright lord of the hours
To weary of thy bloom in sultry bowers;
Nor like the summer rose, that one by one,
Yields her fair, fragrant petals to the sun,
Faint with the envenomed sweetness of his smile,
That doth to lingering death her race beguile;
But, as some spirit of the air doth fade
Into the light from its own essence rayed,
So, Glory of the morning, fair and cold,
Soon in thy circling halo dost thou fold
Thy virgin bloom, and from our vision hide
That form too fair, on earth, unsullied to abide.

EMMA C. EMBURY (1806–1863)

The oldest child of a prominent New York City physician, Emma C. Embury sent in her poems to the *New York Mirror* under the name "Ianthe." Embury began publishing under her own name after her marriage in 1828. Her husband, a bank president, was praised for supporting his wife's writing. Embury was the leader of a literary salon, which included Edgar Allan Poe and Rufus W. Griswold. Embury's poems were published in *Guido, a Tale: Sketches from History and Other Poems*, and in periodicals of her time, including *Godey's Lady's Book*, *The Knickerbocker Magazine*, and *The Ladies' Companion*. Embury's writings—both prose and verse—frequently centered on the themes of love and affection.

The Widow's Wooer

He woos me with those honeyed words
    That women love to hear,
Those gentle flatteries that fall
    So sweet on every ear:
He tells me that my face is fair,
    Too fair for grief to shade;
My cheek, he says, was never meant
    In sorrow's gloom to fade.

He stands beside me when I sing
    The songs of other days,
And whispers, in love's thrilling tones,
    The words of heartfelt praise;
And often in my eyes he looks,
    Some answering love to see;
In vain—he there can only read
    The faith of memory.

He little knows what thoughts awake
    With every gentle word;
How, by his looks and tones, the founts
    Of tenderness are stirred:
The visions of my youth return,
    Joys far too bright to last,
And while he speaks of future bliss,
    I think but of the past.

Like lamps in eastern sepulchres,
    Amid my heart's deep gloom,
Affection sheds its holiest light

Upon my husband's tomb:
And as those lamps, if brought once more
    To upper air grow dim,
So my soul's love is cold and dead,
    Unless it glow for him.

Love Unsought

They tell me that I must not love,
    That thou wilt spurn the free
And unbought tenderness that gives
    Its hidden wealth to thee.
It may be so: I heed it not,
Nor would I change my blissful lot,
When thus I am allowed to make
My heart a bankrupt for thy sake.

They tell me when the fleeting charm
    Of novelty is o'er,
Thou 'lt turn away with careless brow
    And think of me no more.
It may be so! enough for me
If sunny skies still smile o'er thee,
Or I can trace, when thou art far,
Thy pathway like a distant star.

A Portrait

A gentle maiden, whose large loving eyes
    Enshrine a tender, melancholy light,
Like the soft radiance of the starry skies,
    Or Autumn sunshine, mellowed when most bright,
She is not sad, yet in her look appears
Something that makes the gazer think of tears.

She is not beautiful, her features bear
    A loveliness by angel hands impressed,
Such as the pure in heart alone may wear,
    The outward symbol of a soul at rest;
And this beseems her well, for Love and Truth
Companion ever with her guileless youth.

She hath a delicate foot, a dainty hand,
    And every limb displays unconscious grace,

Like one, who, born a lady in the land,
  Taketh no thought how best to fill her place,
But moveth ever at her own sweet will,
While gentleness and pride attend her still.

Nor has she lost, by any sad mischance,
  The happy thoughts that to her years belong—
Her step is ever fleetest in the dance,
  Her voice is ever gayest in the song;
The silent air by her rich notes is stirred,
As by the music of a forest bird.

There dwelleth in the sinlessness of youth
  A sweet rebuke that Vice may not endure;
And thus she makes an atmosphere of truth,
  For all things in her presence grow more pure;
She walks in light—her guardian angel flings
A halo round her from his radiant wings.

ELIZABETH OAKES-SMITH (1806–1893)

One of the first American women to lecture on abolition and women's rights, Oakes-Smith was born in North Yarmouth, Maine. She married a newspaper publisher when she was seventeen and had four sons. In the 1840s, Oakes-Smith edited *The Mayflower*, an annual published in Boston. She also wrote poems, criticisms, and essays under her own name and under the pen name of Ernest Helfenstein. Some of her published works include: *The Sinless Child and Other Poems* (1843), and children's stories such as *The True Child* and *Rosebud* (1845). *Woman and Her Needs* (1851) was originally published as a series in the *New York Tribune*. At the age of forty-five, Oakes-Smith was a public speaker on women's rights, and in 1868, she became a charter member of Sorosis, the first women's club in New York.

Ode to Sappho

Bright, glowing Sappho! child of love and song!
  Adown the blueness of long-distant years
Beams forth thy glorious shape, and steals along
  Thy melting tones, beguiling us to tears.
    Thou priestess of great hearts,
      Thrilled with the secret fire
    By which a god imparts
      The anguish of desire—
  For meaner souls be mean content—
  Thine was a higher element.

Over Leucadia's rock thou leanest yet,
  With thy wild song, and all thy locks outspread;
The stars are in thine eyes, the moon hath set—
  The night dew falls upon thy radiant head;
    And thy resounding lyre—
      Ah! not so wildly sway:
    Thy soulful lips inspire
      And steal our hearts away!
  Swanlike and beautiful, thy dirge
  Still moans along the Ægean surge.

No unrequited love filled thy lone heart,
  But thine infinitude did on thee weigh,
And all the wildness of despair impart,
  Stealing the down from Hope's own wing away.
    Couldst thou not suffer on,
      Bearing the direful pang,

While thy melodious tone
    Through wondering cities rang?
Couldst thou not bear thy godlike grief?
In godlike utterance find relief?

Devotion, fervor, might upon thee wait:
    But what were these to thine? all cold and chill,
And left thy burning heart but desolate;
    Thy wondrous beauty with despair might fill
        The worshipper who bent
        Entrancéd at thy feet:
    Too affluent the dower lent
        Where song and beauty meet!
    Consumed by a Promethean fire
    Wert thou, O daughter of the lyre!

Alone, above Leucadia's wave art thou,
    Most beautiful, most gifted, yet alone!
Ah! what to thee the crown from Pindar's brow?
    What the loud plaudit and the garlands thrown
        By the enraptured throng,
          When thou in matchless grace
        Didst move with lyre and song,
          And monarchs gave thee place?
    What hast thou left, proud one? what token?
    Alas! a lyre and heart—both broken!

The Drowned Mariner

A mariner sat on the shrouds one night;
    The wind was piping free;
Now bright, now dimmed was the moonlight pale,
And the phosphor gleamed in the wake of the whale,
    As he floundered in the sea;
The scud was flying athwart the sky,
The gathering winds went whistling by,
And the wave as it towered, then fell in spray,
Looked an emerald wall in the moonlight ray.

The mariner swayed and rocked on the mast,
    But the tumult pleased him well;
Down the yawning wave his eye he cast,
And the monsters watched as they hurried past

Or lightly rose and fell;
For their broad, damp fins were under the tide,
And they lashed as they passed the vessel's side,
And their filmy eyes, all huge and grim,
Glared fiercely up, and they glared at him.

Now freshens the gale, and the brave ship goes
   Like an uncurbed steed along;
A sheet of flame is the spray she throws,
As her gallant prow the water ploughs,
   But the ship is fleet and strong:
The topsails are reefed and the sails are furled,
And onward she sweeps o'er the watery world,
And dippeth her spars in the surging flood;
But there came no chill to the mariner's blood.

Wildly she rocks, but he swingeth at ease,
   And holds him by the shroud;
And as she careens to the crowding breeze,
The gaping deep the mariner sees,
   And the surging heareth loud.
Was that a face, looking up at him,
With its pallid cheek and its cold eyes dim?
Did it beckon him down? did it call his name?
Now rolleth the ship the way whence it came.

The mariner looked, and he saw with dread
   A face he knew too well;
And the cold eyes glared, the eyes of the dead,
And its long hair out on the wave was spread.
   Was there a tale to tell?
The stout ship rocked with a reeling speed,
And the mariner groaned, as well he need;
For, ever, down as she plunged on her side,
The dead face gleamed from the briny tide.

Bethink thee, mariner, well, of the past,—
   A voice calls loud for thee:—
There's a stifled prayer, the first, the last;—
The plunging ship on her beam is cast,—
   Oh, where shall thy burial be?
Bethink thee of oaths that were lightly spoken,
Bethink thee of vows that were lightly broken,

Bethink thee of all that is dear to thee,
For thou art alone on the raging sea:

Alone in the dark, alone on the wave,
   To buffet the storm alone,
To struggle aghast at thy watery grave,
To struggle and feel there is none to save,—
   God shield thee, helpless one!
The stout limbs yield, for their strength is past,
The trembling hands on the deep are cast,
The white brow gleams a moment more,
Then slowly sinks—the struggle is o'er.

Down, down where the storm is hushed to sleep,
   Where the sea its dirge shall swell,
Where the amber drops for thee shall weep,
And the rose-lipped shell her music keep,
   There thou shalt slumber well.
The gem and the pearl lie heaped at thy side,
They fell from the neck of the beautiful bride,
From the strong man's hand, from the maiden's brow,
As they slowly sunk to the wave below.

A peopled home is the ocean bed;
   The mother and child are there;
The fervent youth and the hoary head,
The maid, with her floating locks outspread,
   The babe with its silken hair;
As the water moveth they lightly sway,
And the tranquil lights on their features play;
And there is each cherished and beautiful form,
Away from decay, and away from the storm.

LUCRETIA DAVIDSON (1808–1825)

Born in Plattsburg, New York, Lucretia Davidson was a precocious youth who learned the alphabet at the age of three. A sickly child, Davidson's health began to worsen in 1823. She wrote her longest poem, "Amir Khan," and a prose story while visiting relatives in Canada. In 1824, Davidson attended Emma Hart Willard's seminary in Troy, New York, and then went to a boarding school in Albany. Her life was short; she died one month shy of her seventeenth birthday and her poems and prose were published after her death. Lucretia's younger sister, Margaret (1823–1838), was only two years old when her sister died. Margaret aspired to follow in Lucretia's footsteps and wrote poems as well. Mirroring her older sister, Margaret, too, died in her teens, just before her sixteenth birthday.

On the Birth of Her Sister Margaret

Sweet babe, I cannot hope thou wilt be freed
From woes, to all, since earliest time, decreed;
But may'st thou be with resignation blessed,
To bear each evil, howsoe'er distressed.

May Hope her anchor lend amid the storm,
And o'er the tempest rear her angel form!
May sweet Benevolence, whose words are peace,
To the rude whirlwinds softly whisper, "Cease!"

And may Religion, Heaven's own darling child,
Teach thee at human cares and griefs to smile;
Teach thee to look beyond this world of woe,
To Heaven's high fount, whence mercies ever flow.

And when this vale of tears is safely passed—
When Death's dark curtain shuts the scene at last—
May thy freed spirit leave this earthly sod,
And fly to seek the bosom of thy God.

America

And this was once the realm of Nature, where
Wild as the wind, though exquisitely fair,
She breathed the mountain breeze, or bowed to kiss
The dimpling waters with unbounded bliss.
Here in this Paradise of earth, where first
Wild mountain Liberty began to burst,
Once Nature's temple rose in simple grace,

47

The hill her throne, the world her dwelling-place.
And where are now her lakes, so still and lone,
Her thousand streams with bending shrubs o'ergrown?
Where her dark cat'racts tumbling from on high,
With rainbow arch aspiring to the sky?
Her tow'ring pines with fadeless wreaths entwined,
Her waving alders streaming to the wind?
Nor these alone,—her own,—her fav'rite child,
All fire, all feeling; man untaught and wild;
Where can the lost, lone son of Nature stray?
For art's high car is rolling on its way;
A wand'rer of the world, he flies to drown
The thoughts of days gone by and pleasures flown
In the deep draught, whose dregs are death and woe,
With slavery's iron chain concealed below.
Once through the tangled wood, with noiseless tread
And throbbing heart, the lurking warrior sped,
Aimed his sure weapon, won the prize, and turned,
While his high heart with wild ambition burned
With song and war-whoop to his native tree,
There on its bark to carve the victory.
His all of learning did that act comprise,
But still in *nature's* volume doubly wise.

The wayward stream which once, with idle bound,
Whirled on resistless in its foaming round,
Now curbed by art flows on, a wat'ry chain
Linking the snow-capped mountains to the main.
Where once the alder in luxuriance grew,
Or the tall pine its towering branches threw
Abroad to heaven, with dark and haughty brow,
There mark the realms of plenty smiling now;
There the full sheaf of Ceres richly glows,
And Plenty's fountain blesses as it flows;
And man, a brute when left to wander wild,
A reckless creature, Nature's lawless child,
What boundless streams of knowledge rolling now
From the full hand of art around him flow!
Improvement strides the surge, while from afar
Learning rolls onward in her silver car;
Freedom unfurls her banner o'er his head,
While peace sleeps sweetly on her native bed.

The Muse arises from the wild-wood glen,
And chants her sweet and hallowed song again,
As in those halcyon days, which bards have sung,
When hope was blushing, and when life was young.
Thus shall she rise, and thus her sons shall rear
Her sacred temple *here*, and only *here*,
While Percival, her loved and chosen priest,
Forever blessing, though himself unblest,
Shall fan the fire that blazes at her shrine,
And charm the ear with numbers half divine.

MARGARET FULLER (1810–1850)

Tutored by her father in Cambridgeport, Massachusetts, Margaret Fuller was fluent in four foreign languages. Through her friendship with Ralph Waldo Emerson, she became editor of *The Dial*, a Transcendentalist magazine, and began to give public speeches in Boston on furthering women's education. At Horace Greeley's invitation, Fuller worked as a literary critic for the *New York Tribune*, and in 1845 she published the classic work *Woman in the Nineteenth Century*. Fuller spent some time in Europe, becoming the first American woman to work as a foreign correspondent. She married an Italian nobleman in 1849 and, when she was returning to the U.S. in 1850, Fuller, her husband, and their child died in a shipwreck off Fire Island, New York.

Flaxman

We deemed the secret lost, the spirit gone,
Which spake in Greek simplicity of thought,
And in the forms of gods and heroes wrought
Eternal beauty from the sculptured stone,—
A higher charm than modern culture won
With all the wealth of metaphysic lore,
Gifted to analyze, dissect, explore.
A many-colored light flows from one sun;
Art, 'neath its beams, a motley thread has spun;
The prism modifies the perfect day;
But thou hast known such mediums to shun,
And cast once more on life a pure, white ray.
Absorbed in the creations of thy mind,
Forgetting daily self, my truest self I find.

Instrumental Music

The charms of melody, in simple airs,
  By human voices sung, are always felt;
  With thoughts responsive careless hearers melt,
Of secret ills, which our frail nature bears.
  We listen, weep, forget. But when the throng
Of a great master's thoughts, above the reach
Of words or colors, wire and wood can teach
  By laws which to the spirit-world belong—
When several parts, to tell one mood combined,
  Flash meaning on us we can ne'er express.
Giving to matter subtlest powers of mind,
  Superior joys attentive souls confess:
The harmony which suns and stars obey,
Blesses our earth-bound state with visions of supernal day.

ELIZABETH CLEMENTINE KINNEY
(1810–1889)

Poet and essayist Elizabeth Clementine Kinney was born in New York City. Her poems appeared in *Knickerbocker Magazine*, *Graham's Magazine*, and others. She is the mother of poet and critic Edmund Clarence Stedman, and wrote *Felicita* (1855), a verse romance, and *Poems* (1867). She lived in New Jersey for a time and then moved to Europe, where she remained for fourteen years. Kinney was a close friend of the Brownings, and was considered a leader in both American and English literary circles.

A Dream

'Twas summer, and the spot a cool retreat—
Where curious eyes came not, nor footstep rude
Disturbed the lovers' chosen solitude:
Beneath an oak there was a mossy seat,
Where we reclined, while birds above us wooed
Their mates in songs voluptuously sweet.
A limpid brook went murmuring by our feet,
And all conspired to urge the tender mood.
Methought I touched the streamlet with a flower,
When from its bosom sprang a fountain clear,
Falling again in the translucent shower
Which made more green each blade of grass appear:
"This stream's thy heart," I said; "Love's touch alone
Can change it to the fount which maketh green my own."

FRANCES SARGENT OSGOOD (1811–1850)

As a child in Hingham, Massachusetts, Frances Sargent Osgood submitted poems to Lydia Maria Child's *Juvenile Miscellany*. Osgood married in 1835 and gave birth to her first daughter, Ellen, whom she often included in her sentimental poems. Osgood and her husband lived in London in the late 1830s, and she published two books of poetry there. She wrote and edited six books in the 1840s, including *The Poetry of Flowers and Flowers of Poetry* (1841) and *Poems* (1846). Osgood also attended meetings at New York's literary salons, and was soon acquainted with Edgar Allan Poe, who published her poems regularly in the *Broadway Journal*. After her third daughter died in infancy, Osgood became ill and died of tuberculosis in 1850.

Ellen Learning to Walk

My beautiful trembler! how wildly she shrinks!
    And how wistful she looks while she lingers!
Papa is extremely uncivil, she thinks,—
    She but pleaded for one of his fingers!

What eloquent pleading! the hand reaching out,
    As if doubting so strange a refusal;
While her blue eyes say plainly, "What is he about
    That he does not assist me as usual?"

Come on, my pet Ellen! we won't let you slip,—
    Unclasp those soft arms from his knee, love;
I see a faint smile round that exquisite lip,
    A smile half reproach and half glee, love.

So! that's my brave baby! one foot falters forward,
    Half doubtful the other steals by it!
What, shrinking again! why, you shy little coward!
    'Twon't kill you to walk a bit!—try it!

There! steady, my darling! huzza! I have caught her!
    I clasp her, caress'd and caressing!
And she hides her bright face, as if what we had taught her
    Were something to blush for—the blessing!

Now back again! Bravo! that shout of delight,
    How it thrills to the hearts that adore her!
Joy, joy for her mother! and blest be the night
    When her little light feet first upbore her!

A Dancing Girl

She comes—the spirit of the dance!
  And but for those large, eloquent eyes,
Where passion speaks in every glance,
  She'd seem a wanderer from the skies.

So light that, gazing breathless there,
  Lest the celestial dream should go,
You'd think the music in the air
  Waved the fair vision to and fro!

Or that the melody's sweet flow
  Within the radiant creature played,
And those soft wreathing arms of snow
  And white sylph feet the music made.

Now gliding slow with dreamy grace,
  Her eyes beneath their lashes lost,
Now motionless, with lifted face,
  And small hands on her bosom crossed.

And now with flashing eyes she springs,—
  Her whole bright figure raised in air,
As if her soul had spread its wings
  And poised her one wild instant there!

She spoke not; but, so richly fraught
  With language are her glance and smile,
That, when the curtain fell, I thought
  She had been talking all the while.

Ah! Woman Still

  Ah! woman still
  Must veil the shrine,
Where feeling feeds the fire divine,
  Nor sing at will,
  Untaught by art,
The music prison'd in her heart!
  Still gay the note,
  And light the lay,
The woodbird warbles on the spray,
  Afar to float;

But homeward flown,
Within his nest, how changed the tone!

Oh! none can know,
Who have not heard
The music-soul that thrills the bird,
The carol low
As coo of dove
He warbles to his woodland-love!
The world would say
'Twas vain and wild,
The impassion'd lay of Nature's child;
And Feeling so
Should veil the shrine
Where softly glow her fires divine!

HARRIET BEECHER STOWE (1812–1896)

Daughter of clergyman Lyman Beecher, Harriet Beecher Stowe soared to fame with her antislavery novel, *Uncle Tom's Cabin* (1852), which sold 300,000 copies in its first year. It was originally published in the *National Era* as a serialized story in 1851–2. Born in Connecticut, Stowe became a teacher in the seminary founded by her sister, Catherine Beecher. After marrying a professor in 1836, she contributed stories, articles, and poems to periodicals to augment their small income. Stowe's home was directly involved in the Underground Railroad, and her powerful Civil War book intensified the abolitionists' struggle. In 1853, Stowe published *A Key to Uncle Tom's Cabin*, which contained authentic evidence on the evils of slavery. She also published *Sunny Memories of Foreign Lands* (1854) and another antislavery book, *Dred: A Tale of the Great Dismal Swamp* (1856).

The Other World

It lies around us like a cloud,
    The world we do not see;
Yet the sweet closing of an eye
    May bring us there to be.

Its gentle breezes fan our cheeks
    Amid our worldly cares;
Its gentle voices whisper love,
    And mingle with our prayers.

Sweet hearts around us throb and beat,
    Sweet helping hands are stirred,
And palpitates the veil between,
    With breathings almost heard.

The silence, awful, sweet, and calm,
    They have no power to break;
For mortal words are not for them
    To utter or partake.

So thin, so soft, so sweet they glide,
    So near to press they seem,
They lull us gently to our rest,
    They melt into our dream.

And, in the hush of rest they bring,
    'T is easy now to see
How lovely and how sweet a pass
    The hour of death may be;—

To close the eye and close the ear,
  Wrapped in a trance of bliss,
And, gently drawn in loving arms,
  To swoon from that to this: —

Scarce knowing if we wake or sleep,
  Scarce asking where we are,
To feel all evil sink away,
  All sorrow and all care!

Sweet souls around us! watch us still,
  Press nearer to our side;
Into our thoughts, into our prayers,
  With gentle helping glide.

Let death between us be as naught,
  A dried and vanished stream;
Your joy be the reality,
  Our suffering life the dream.

MARY E. HEWITT (1818?–1894)

One of the more obscure women poets, Mary E. Hewitt (Stebbins) was born in Malden, Massachusetts. Popular in her time, Hewitt's poetry has been overlooked in anthologies of nineteenth-century poets. Hewitt moved to New York with her first husband, James L. Hewitt, a music publisher. Her verses first appeared in *Knickerbocker Magazine* under the pseudonyms "Ione" and "Jane." In the 1840s and 1850s, Hewitt was at the apex of her fame, publishing her dramatic poetry in various periodicals and in books such as *The Songs of Our Land, and Other Poems* (1845), reissued in 1853 as *Poems: Sacred, Passionate, and Legendary*. She also published a biography of Frances Sargent Osgood in 1850 and *Heroines of History* (1856), a series of prose sketches.

Imitation of Sappho

If to repeat thy name when none may hear me,
    To find thy thought with all my thoughts inwove;
To languish where thou'rt not—to sigh when near thee:
    Oh, if this be to love thee, I do love!

If when thou utterest low words of greeting,
    To feel through every vein the torrent pour;
Then back again the hot tide swift retreating,
    Leave me all powerless, silent as before:

If to list breathless to thine accents falling,
    Almost to pain, upon my eager ear—
And fondly when alone to be recalling
    The words that I would die again to hear:

If 'neath thy glance my heart all strength forsaking,
    Pant in my breast as pants the frighted dove;
If to think on thee ever, sleeping—waking—
    Oh! if this be to love thee, I do love!

Harold the Valiant

I mid 'the hills was born,
    Where the skilled bowmen
Send with unerring shaft
    Death to the foemen.
But I love to steer my bark—
    To fear a stranger—
Over the Maelstrom's edge,

Daring the danger;
And where the mariner
    Paleth affrighted,
Over the sunken rocks
    I dash on delighted.
The far waters know my keel,
    No tide restrains me;
But ah! a Russian maid
    Coldly disdains me.

Once round Sicilia's isle
    Sailed I, unfearing:
Conflict was on my prow,
    Glory was steering.
Where fled the stranger ship
    Wildly before me,
Down, like the hungry hawk,
    My vessel bore me;
We carved on the craven's deck
    The red runes of slaughter:
When my bird whets her beak
    I give no quarter.
The far waters know my keel,
    No tide restrains me;
But ah! a Russian maid
    Coldly disdains me.

Countless as spears of grain
    Stood the warriors of Drontheim,
When like the hurricane
    I swept down upon them!
Like chaff beneath the flail
    They fell in their numbers:—
Their king with the golden hair
    I sent to his slumbers.
I love the combat fierce,
    No fear restrains me;
But ah! a Russian maid
    Coldly disdains me.

Once o'er the Baltic Sea
    Swift we were dashing;

Bright on our twenty spears
   Sunlight was flashing;
When through the Skager Rack
   The storm-wind was driven,
And from our bending mast
   The broad sail was riven:
Then, while the angry brine
   Foamed like a flagon,
Brimful the yesty rime
   Filled our brown dragon;
But I, with sinewy hand
   Strengthened in slaughter,
Forth from the straining ship
   Bailed the dun water.
The wild waters know my keel,
   No storm restrains me;
But ah! a Russian maid
   Coldly disdains me.

Firmly I curb my steed,
   As e'er Thracian horseman;
My hand throws the javelin true,
   Pride of the Norseman;
And the bold skater marks,
   While his lips quiver,
Where o'er the bending ice
   I skim the river:
Forth to my rapid oar
   The boat swiftly springeth—
Springs like the mettled steed
   When the spur stingeth.
Valiant I am in fight,
   No fear restrains me;
But ah! a Russian maid
   Coldly disdains me.

Saith she, the maiden fair,
   The Norsemen are cravens?
I in the Southland gave
   A feast to the ravens!
Green lay the sward outspread,
   The bright sun was o'er us

When the strong fighting men
   Rushed down before us.
Midway to meet the shock
   My courser bore me,
And like Thor's hammer crashed
   My strong hand before me;
Left we their maids in tears,
   Their city in embers:
The sound of the Viking's spears
   The Southland remembers!
I love the combat fierce,
   No fear restrains me;
But ah! a Russian maid
   Coldly disdains me.

JULIA WARD HOWE (1819–1910)

Born into a well-to-do family in New York City, Julia Ward Howe was prominent during the Civil War, thanks to her poem "Battle Hymn of the Republic." Sung to the tune of "John Brown's Body," the famous poem, written in 1861 while visiting an army camp, became the war song of the Union army. Howe lectured on women's suffrage, prison reform, and international peace. She and her humanitarian husband published the *Commonwealth*, an abolitionist newspaper. *Passion Flowers* (1854), *Words for the Hour* (1857), and *Later Lyrics* (1866) are some of Howe's books of poems. In 1870, Howe published "Appeal to Womanhood Throughout the World," urging an international meeting of women on the subject of peace; she achieved this one year later. She also wrote biographies, travel books, and essays, and was the first woman to be elected to the American Academy of Arts and Letters.

Battle Hymn of the Republic

Mine eyes have seen the glory of the coming of the Lord:
He is trampling out the vintage where the grapes of wrath are stored;
He hath loosed the fateful lightning of his terrible swift sword:
    His truth is marching on.

I have seen Him in the watch-fires of a hundred circling camps;
They have builded Him an altar in the evening dews and damps;
I can read His righteous sentence by the dim and flaring lamps.
    His day is marching on.

I have read a fiery gospel, writ in burnished rows of steel:
"As ye deal with my contemners, so with you my grace shall deal;
Let the Hero, born of woman, crush the serpent with his heel,
    Since God is marching on."

He has sounded forth the trumpet that shall never call retreat;
He is sifting out the hearts of men before his judgment-seat:
Oh! be swift, my soul, to answer Him! be jubilant, my feet!
    Our God is marching on.

In the beauty of the lilies Christ was born across the sea,
With a glory in his bosom that transfigures you and me:
As he died to make men holy, let us die to make men free,
    While God is marching on.

My Last Dance

The shell of objects inwardly consumed
Will stand till some convulsive wind awakes;
Such sense hath Fire to waste the heart of things,
Nature such love to hold the form she makes.

Thus wasted joys will show their early bloom,
Yet crumble at the breath of a caress;
The golden fruitage hides the scathèd bough;
Snatch it, thou scatterest wide its emptiness.

For pleasure bidden, I went forth last night
To where, thick hung, the festal torches gleamed;
Here were the flowers, the music, as of old;
Almost the very olden time it seemed.

For one with cheek unfaded (though he brings
My buried brothers to me in his look)
Said, 'Will you dance?' At the accustomed words
I gave my hand, the old position took.

Sound, gladsome measure! at whose bidding once
I felt the flush of pleasure to my brow,
While my soul shook the burthen of the flesh,
And in its young pride said, 'Lie lightly, thou!'

Then, like a gallant swimmer, flinging high
My breast against the golden waves of sound,
I rode the madd'ning tumult of the dance,
Mocking fatigue, that never could be found.

Chide not—it was not vanity, nor sense,
(The brutish scorn such vaporous delight,)
But Nature, cadencing her joy of strength
To the harmonious limits of her right.

She gave her impulse to the dancing Hours,
To winds that weep, to stars that noiseless turn;
She marked the measure rapid hearts must keep,
Devised each pace that glancing feet should learn.

And sure, that prodigal o'erflow of life,
Unvowed as yet to family or state,
Sweet sounds, white garments, flowery coronals
Make holy in the pageant of our fate.

Sound, measure! but to stir my heart no more—
For, as I moved to join the dizzy race,
My youth fell from me; all its blooms were gone,
And others showed them, smiling, in my face.

Faintly I met the shock of circling forms
Linked each to other, Fashion's galley-slaves,
Dream-wondering, like an unaccustomed ghost
That starts, surprised, to stumble over graves.

For graves were 'neath my feet, whose placid masks
Smiled out upon my folly mournfully,
While all the host of the departed said,
'Tread lightly—thou art ashes, even as we.'

Woman

A vestal priestess, proudly pure,
    But of a meek and quiet spirit;
With soul all dauntless to endure,
    And mood so calm that naught can stir it,
Save when a thought most deeply thrilling
Her eyes with gentlest tears is filling,
Which seem with her true words to start
From the deep fountain at her heart.

A mien that neither seeks nor shuns
    The homage scattered in her way;
A love that hath few favored ones,
    And yet for all can work and pray;
A smile wherein each mortal reads
The very sympathy he needs;
An eye like to a mystic book
    Of lays that bard or prophet sings,
Which keepeth for the holiest look
    Of holiest love its deepest things.

A form to which a king had bent,
The fireside's dearest ornament—
Known in the dwellings of the poor
Better than at the rich man's door;
A life that ever onward goes,
Yet in itself has deep repose.

A vestal priestess, maid, or wife—
   Vestal, and vowed to offer up
The innocence of a holy life
   To Him who gives the mingled cup;
With man its bitter sweets to share,
To live and love, to do and dare;
His prayer to breathe, his tears to shed,
Breaking to him the heavenly bread
Of hopes which, all too high for earth,
Have yet in her a mortal birth.

This is the woman I have dreamed,
And to my childish thought she seemed
The woman I myself should be:
Alas! I would that I were she.

The Burial of Schlesinger

Sad music breathes upon the air,
   And steps come mournfully and slow;
Heavy is the load we bear,
Fellow-men our burthen share,
   Death has laid our brother low.
Ye have heard our joyous strain,
   Listen to our notes of wo!

     Do ye not remember him
   Whose finger, from the thrilling wire,
   Now drew forth tears, now tones of fire?
Ah! that hand is cold for ever:
Gone is now life's fitful fever—
     We sing his requiem.

We are singing him to rest—
   He will rise a spirit blest.
     Sing it softly, sing it slowly—
Let each note our sorrow tell,
For it is our last farewell,
     And his grave is lone and lowly.

   We sorrow for thee, brother!
     We grieve that thou must lie
Far from the spot where thy fathers sleep;

Thou camest o'er the briny deep
   In a stranger land to die.

  We bear thee gently, brother,
    To thy last resting-place;
Soon shall the earth above thee close,
And the dark veil of night repose
    For ever on thy face.

  We placed the last flowers, brother,
    Upon thy senseless brow;
We kissed that brow before 't was hid,
We wept upon thy coffin-lid,
    But all unmoved wert thou.

We've smoothed the green turf, brother,
    Above thy lowly head;
Earth in her breast receive thee:
Oh, it is sad to leave thee,
    Alone in thy narrow bed!

Thou art not with us, brother—
    Yet, in yon blissful land,
Perhaps, thou still canst hear us—
Perhaps thou hoverest near us
    And smilest as the choral band,
    Which once obeyed thy master hand,
Now linger with their tears to leave
The sod that seals thy grave.

The sun is sinking, brother,
    And with it our melody.
The dying cadence of our rite
Is mingled with the dying light.
    Oh, brother! by that fading ray,
    And by this mournful parting lay,
    We will remember thee.

The sculptor, in his chiselled stone,
    The painter, in his colors blent,
The bard, in numbers all his own,
    Raises himself his monument:
But he, whose every touch could wake

A passion, and a thought control,
He who, to bless the ear, did make
  Music of his very soul;
Who bound for us, in golden chains,
  The golden links of harmony—
Naught is left us of his strains,
  Naught but their fleeting memory:
Then, while a trace of him remains,
  Shall we not cherish it tenderly?

ALICE CARY (1820–1871)

The fourth of nine children, Alice Cary's first poem was published in a Cincinnati newspaper when she was eighteen years old. Alice shared a love of literature with her sister, Phoebe, and together, the sisters published a volume of poems in 1850. Alice, considered the better poet of the two, comprised two-thirds of the book. The financial success of the book enabled them to move to New York City, where they contributed to periodicals. Alice's books include *Clovernook Papers* (1852 and 1853), *Lyra and Other Poems* (1852), a children's book, and several novels. She was also the first president of Sorosis, the pioneer women's club founded by Jane Croly.

The Sea-Side Cave

"A bird of the air shall carry the voice, and that
which hath wings shall tell the matter."

At the dead of night by the side of the Sea
I met my gray-haired enemy,—
The glittering light of his serpent eye
Was all I had to see him by.

At the dead of night, and stormy weather
We went into a cave together,—
Into a cave by the side of the Sea,
And—he never came out with me!

The flower that up through the April mould
Comes like a miser dragging his gold,
Never made spot of earth so bright
As was the ground in the cave that night.

Dead of night, and stormy weather!
Who should see us going together
Under the black and dripping stone
Of the cave from whence I came alone!

Next day as my boy sat on my knee
He picked the gray hairs off from me,
And told with eyes brimful of fear
How a bird in the meadow near

Over her clay-built nest had spread
Sticks and leaves all bloody red,
Brought from a cave by the side of the Sea
Where some murdered man must be.

To Solitude

I am weary of the working,
  Weary of the long day's heat;
To thy comfortable bosom,
  Wilt thou take me, spirit sweet?

Weary of the long, blind struggle
  For a pathway bright and high,—
Weary of the dimly dying
  Hopes that never quite all die.

Weary searching a bad cipher
  For a good that must be meant;
Discontent with being weary,—
  Weary with my discontent.

I am weary of the trusting
  Where my trusts but torments prove;
Wilt thou keep faith with me? wilt thou
  Be my true and tender love?

I am weary drifting, driving
  Like a helmless bark at sea;
Kindly, comfortable spirit,
  Wilt thou give thyself to me?

Give thy birds to sing me sonnets?
  Give thy winds my cheeks to kiss?
And thy mossy rocks to stand for
  The memorials of our bliss?

I in reverence will hold thee,
  Never vexed with jealous ills,
Though thy wild and wimpling waters
  Wind about a thousand hills.

FANNY CROSBY (1820–1915)

Primarily known as a hymn writer, Frances Jane (Fanny) Crosby lost her sight to an eye infection when she was six weeks old. Born in Putnam County, New York, Crosby attended the New York Institution for the Blind. She published her verses in the *New York Herald* and other newspapers in the 1840s. After her first two volumes, *The Blind Girl and Other Poems* (1844) and *Monterey and Other Poems* (1851), she began to write verses to be set to music. She taught English grammar and ancient history at the New York Institution for the Blind, and married a blind music teacher at the school in 1858. Since Crosby used nearly 200 different pseudonyms, she is estimated to have written approximately 6,000 hymns in her lifetime; among her most famous is "Safe in the Arms of Jesus."

Voice of the Flowers

Ye have a kind voice, sweet flowers!
    Of pure angelic tone;
It has no echo in greenwood bowers,
    But speaks to the heart alone.

Ye have looked on the blush of day,
    And stolen its rosy hue;
But the fountain and song-bird's lay
    Are silent, alas! to you.

No clambering vines caress
    Your artless forms so fair;
Your velvet leaves are motionless,
    For beauty is sleeping there.

And the flower-spirit hovers near,
    And bears on its dove-like wing,
A gem that was once a pearly tear
    On the infant cheek of spring.

Ye have a sad voice, sweet flowers!
    That whispers of quick decay;
The garlands worn in happiest hours
    Are the soonest to pass away.

I know that the frost of death
    Ere long will silently chill;
But the fragrance exhaling now
    Will linger around me still.

And thus doth a smile, the last
  By the lips of a fond friend given,
A fragrance shed though that friend hath passed
  To his home in the starry heaven.

The Dead Child

She sat alone beside the couch of death,
And looked upon the features of her child;
The silken curls lay on its velvet cheek,
And as she stooped to kiss those parted lips
From which the ruby tints had scarcely fled,
It seemed as if her own sweet lullaby
Had hushed it to a soft and gentle sleep.
She clasped its little hands upon its breast,
And then in melancholy accents said:—
Oh no! it cannot be, thou art not dead!
Look up, my daughter! let me see again
Those laughing eyes in their long lashes hid;
'Tis hard to give thee up, in one short hour
To feel the hopes of years for ever crushed,
And severed one by one, those tender cords
That round the fibres of my heart were twined,
Till with my very life they seemed to blend.
Oh! there are wounds which time alone must heal,
And tears which only heaven can wipe away.
Thy mother's hand a pencil sketch shall draw
Of thee, my child, so beautiful and young;
For I would keep thine image near me still.
A moment, and the painful task begun,
She had been weeping bitterly, but now
All trace of tears had vanished from her cheek;
And she prayed earnestly to God for strength.
Nor was that prayer unheard. A still small voice
Had whispered consolation to her heart;
A hand unseen, to firmness nerved her own,
And soon her infant's picture was complete.

PHOEBE CARY (1824–1871)

The younger sister of Alice Cary, Phoebe Cary regularly contributed poems to various periodicals. After the success of their 1850 book, *Poems of Alice and Phoebe Cary*, Phoebe joined her sister in New York. Her religious poem "Nearer Home" became quite a popular hymn, and was better known by its first line: "One sweetly solemn thought." Phoebe's poetry was published in two volumes, *Poems and Parodies* (1854) and *Poems of Faith, Hope, and Love* (1868). A proponent of the women's rights movement, Phoebe worked briefly as an assistant editor of *Revolution*, Susan B. Anthony's paper. Phoebe died of malaria on July 31, 1871, six months after the death of her older sister, Alice.

Nearer Home

One sweetly solemn thought
   Comes to me o'er and o'er;
I am nearer home to-day
   Than I ever have been before;

Nearer my Father's house,
   Where the many mansions be;
Nearer the great white throne,
   Nearer the crystal sea;

Nearer the bound of life,
   Where we lay our burdens down;
Nearer leaving the cross,
   Nearer gaining the crown.

But lying darkly between,
   Winding down through the night,
Is the silent, unknown stream,
   That leads at last to the light.

Closer and closer my steps
   Come to the dread abysm:
Closer Death to my lips
   Presses the awful chrism.

Oh, if my mortal feet
   Have almost gained the brink;
If it be I am nearer home
   Even to-day than I think;

Father, perfect my trust;
   Let my spirit feel in death,

That her feet are firmly set
On the rock of a living faith!

Advice Gratis to Certain Women

By a Woman

O, my strong-minded sisters, aspiring to vote,
And to row with your brothers, all in the same boat,
When you come out to speak to the public your mind,
Leave your tricks, and your airs, and your graces behind!

For instance, when you by the world would be seen
As reporter, or editor (first-class, I mean),
I think—just to come to the point in one line—
What you write will be finer, if 'tis not too fine.

Pray, don't let the thread of your subject be strung
With "golden," and "shimmer," "sweet," "filter," and "flung;"
Nor compel, by your style, all your readers to guess
You've been looking up words Webster marks *obs*.

And another thing: whatever else you may say,
Do keep personalities out of the way;
Don't try every sentence to make people see
What a dear, charming creature the writer must be!

Leave out affectations and pretty appeals;
Don't "drag yourself in by the neck and the heels,"
Your dear little boots, and your gloves; and take heed,
Nor pull your curls over men's eyes while they read.

Don't mistake me; I mean that the public's not home,
You must do as the Romans do, when you're in Rome;
I would have you be womanly, while you are wise;
'Tis the weak and the womanish tricks I despise.

On the other hand: don't write and dress in such styles
As astonish the natives, and frighten the isles;
Do look, on the platform, so folks in the show
Needn't ask, "Which are lions, and which tigers?" you know!

'Tis a good thing to write, and to rule in the state,
But to be a true, womanly woman is great:
And if ever you come to be that, 'twill be when
You can cease to be babies, nor try to be men!

LUCY LARCOM (1824–1893)

Lucy Larcom of Beverly, Massachusetts, began writing poems when she was seven and worked in a mill when she was only eleven. She contributed verse to magazines and published her first book, a series of prose poems, *Similitudes from Ocean and Prairie*, in 1854. In the same year, her poem "Call to Kansas" won a prize from the New England Emigrant Aid Company. She taught college from 1854 to 1862, and edited *Our Folks Magazine* from 1865–73. Larcom published *Childhood Songs* (1873), *Idyl of Work* (1875), a blank verse narrative of mill life, and *A New England Girlhood* (1889), an autobiographical story. Along with John Greenleaf Whittier, Larcom edited the anthologies *Child Life* (1871) and *Songs of Three Centuries* (1883).

Plant a Tree

He who plants a tree
   Plants a hope.
   Rootlets up through fibres blindly grope;
Leaves unfold into horizons free.
   So man's life must climb
   From the clods of time
   Unto heavens sublime.
Canst thou prophesy, thou little tree,
What the glory of thy boughs shall be?

He who plants a tree
   Plants a joy;
   Plants a comfort that will never cloy;
Every day a fresh reality,
   Beautiful and strong,
   To whose shelter throng
   Creatures blithe with song.
If thou couldst but know, thou happy tree,
Of the bliss that shall inhabit thee!

He who plants a tree,—
   He plants peace.
   Under its green curtains jargons cease.
Leaf and zephyr murmur soothingly;
   Shadows soft with sleep
   Down tired eyelids creep,
   Balm of slumber deep.
Never hast thou dreamed, thou blessèd tree,
Of the benediction thou shalt be.

He who plants a tree,—
   He plants youth;
   Vigor won for centuries in sooth;
Life of time, that hints eternity!
   Boughs their strength uprear;
   New shoots, every year,
   On old growths appear;
Thou shalt teach the ages, sturdy tree,
Youth of soul is immortality.

He who plants a tree,—
   He plants love,
   Tents of coolness spreading out above
Wayfarers he may not live to see.
   Gifts that grow are best;
   Hands that bless are blest;
   Plant! life does the rest!
Heaven and earth help him who plants a tree,
And his work its own reward shall be.

A Strip of Blue

I do not own an inch of land,
   But all I see is mine,—
The orchard and the mowing-fields,
   The lawns and gardens fine.
The winds my tax-collectors are,
   They bring me tithes divine,—
Wild scents and subtle essences,
   A tribute rare and free;
And, more magnificent than all,
   My window keeps for me
A glimpse of blue immensity,—
   A little strip of sea.

Richer am I than he who owns
   Great fleets and argosies;
I have a share in every ship
   Won by the inland breeze,
To loiter on yon airy road
   Above the apple-trees.
I freight them with my untold dreams;
   Each bears my own picked crew;

And nobler cargoes wait for them
 Than ever India knew,—
My ships that sail into the East
 Across that outlet blue.

Sometimes they seem like living shapes,—
 The people of the sky,—
Guests in white raiment coming down
 From heaven, which is close by;
I call them by familiar names,
 As one by one draws nigh.
So white, so light, so spirit-like,
 From violet mists they bloom!
The aching wastes of the unknown
 Are half reclaimed from gloom,
Since on life's hospitable sea
 All souls find sailing-room.

The ocean grows a weariness
 With nothing else in sight;
Its east and west, its north and south,
 Spread out from morn till night;
We miss the warm, caressing shore,
 Its brooding shade and light.
A part is greater than the whole;
 By hints are mysteries told.
The fringes of eternity,—
 God's sweeping garment-fold,
In that bright shred of glittering sea,
 I reach out for and hold.

The sails, like flakes of roseate pearl,
 Float in upon the mist;
The waves are broken precious stones,—
 Sapphire and amethyst
Washed from celestial basement walls,
 By suns unsetting kist.
Out through the utmost gates of space,
 Past where the gray stars drift,
To the widening Infinite, my soul
 Glides on, a vessel swift,
Yet loses not her anchorage
 In yonder azure rift.

Here sit I, as a little child;
   The threshold of God's door
Is that clear band of chrysoprase;
   Now the vast temple floor,
The blinding glory of the dome
   I bow my head before.
Thy universe, O God, is home,
   In height or depth, to me;
Yet here upon thy footstool green
   Content am I to be;
Glad when is oped unto my need
   Some sea-like glimpse of Thee.

FRANCES E. W. HARPER (1825–1911)

The daughter of free black parents, Frances E. W. Harper attended Watkins Academy, a school her uncle founded for black children. She worked as a seamstress in Baltimore, and published her first volume of poems, *Forest Leaves*. In 1850, Harper was the first woman instructor at a school in Ohio for free blacks. Active as a lecturer on women's suffrage and abolitionism, Harper also donated money to the Underground Railroad. Her book, *Poems on Miscellaneous Subjects* (1854), made her the most famous black woman poet of her time. She also wrote four novels, which were originally published serially in periodicals. She was named director of the American Association of Education of Colored Youth in 1894, and became vice-president of the National Association of Colored Women in 1897.

Learning to Read

Very soon the Yankee teachers
    Came down and set up school;
But, oh! how the Rebs did hate it,—
    It was agin' their rule.

Our masters always tried to hide
    Book learning from our eyes;
Knowledge did'nt agree with slavery—
    'Twould make us all too wise.

But some of us would try to steal
    A little from the book,
And put the words together,
    And learn by hook or crook.

I remember Uncle Caldwell,
    Who took pot liquor fat
And greased the pages of his book,
    And hid it in his hat.

And had his master ever seen
    The leaves upon his head,
He'd have thought them greasy papers,
    But nothing to be read.

And there was Mr. Turner's Ben,
    Who heard the children spell,
And picked the words right up by heart,
    And learned to read 'em well.

Well, the Northern folks kept sending
    The Yankee teachers down;
And they stood right up and helped us,
    Though Rebs did sneer and frown.

And I longed to read my Bible,
    For precious words it said;
But when I begun to learn it,
    Folks just shook their heads,

And said there is no use trying,
    Oh! Chloe, you're too late;
But as I was rising sixty,
    I had no time to wait.

So I got a pair of glasses,
    And straight to work I went,
And never stopped till I could read
    The hymns and Testament.

Then I got a little cabin
    A place to call my own—
And I felt as independent
    As the queen upon her throne.

The Slave Mother

Heard you that shriek? It rose
    So wildly on the air,
It seem'd as if a burden'd heart
    Was breaking in despair.

Saw you those hands so sadly clasped—
    The bowed and feeble head—
The shuddering of that fragile form—
    That look of grief and dread?

Saw you the sad, imploring eye?
    Its every glance was pain,
As if a storm of agony
    Were sweeping through the brain.

She is a mother pale with fear,
    Her boy clings to her side,

And in her kyrtle vainly tries
　　His trembling form to hide.

He is not hers, although she bore
　　For him a mother's pains;
He is not hers, although her blood
　　Is coursing through his veins!

He is not hers, for cruel hands
　　May rudely tear apart
The only wreath of household love
　　That binds her breaking heart.

The Slave Auction

The sale began—young girls were there,
　　Defenceless in their wretchedness,
Whose stifled sobs of deep despair
　　Revealed their anguish and distress.

And mothers stood, with streaming eyes,
　　And saw their dearest children sold;
Unheeded rose their bitter cries,
　　While tyrants barter'd them for gold.

And woman, with her love and truth—
　　For these in sable forms may dwell—
Gaz'd on the husband of her youth,
　　With anguish none may paint or tell.

And men, whose sole crime was their hue,
　　The impress of their Maker's hand,
And frail and shrinking children too,
　　Were gathered in that mournful band.

Ye who have laid your lov'd to rest,
　　And wept above their lifeless clay,
Know not the anguish of that breast,
　　Whose lov'd are rudely torn away.

Ye may not know how desolate
　　Are bosoms rudely forced to part,
And how a dull and heavy weight
　　Will press the life-drops from the heart.

A Double Standard

Do you blame me that I loved him?
  If when standing all alone
I cried for bread, a careless world
  Pressed to my lips a stone?

Do you blame me that I loved him,
  That my heart beat glad and free,
When he told me in the sweetest tones
  He loved but only me?

Can you blame me that I did not see,
  Beneath his burning kiss,
The serpent's wiles, nor even less hear
  The deadly adder hiss?

Can you blame me that my heart grew cold,
  That the tempted, tempter turned—
When he was feted and caressed
  And I was coldly spurned?

Would you blame him, when you drew from me
  Your dainty robes aside,
If he with gilded baits should claim
  Your fairest as his bride?

Would you blame the world if it should press
  On him a civic crown;
And see me struggling in the depth,
  Then harshly press me down?

Crime has no sex and yet today
  I wear the brand of shame;
Whilst he amid the gay and proud
  Still bears an honored name.

Can you blame me if I've learned to think
  Your hate of vice a sham,
When you so coldly crushed me down,
  And then excused the man?

Yes, blame me for my downward course,
  But oh! remember well,
Within your homes you press the hand
  That led me down to hell!

I'm glad God's ways are not your ways,
　He does not see as man;
Within his love I know there's room
　For those whom others ban.

I think before His great white throne,
　His theme of spotless light,
That whited sepulchres shall wear
　The hue of endless night.

That I who fell, and he who sinned,
　Shall reap as we have sown;
That each the burden of his loss
　Must bear and bear alone.

No golden weights can turn the scale
　Of justice in His sight;
And what is wrong in woman's life
　In man's cannot be right.

She's Free!

How say that by law we may torture and chase
A woman whose crime is the hue of her face?—
With her step on the ice, and her arm on her child,
The danger was fearful, the pathway was wild. . . .
But she's free! yes, free from the land where the slave,
From the hand of oppression, must rest in the grave;
Where bondage and blood, where scourges and chains,
Have placed on our banner indelible stains. . . .
The bloodhounds have miss'd the scent of her way,
The hunter is rifled and foiled of his prey,
The cursing of men and clanking of chains
Make sounds of strange discord on Liberty's plains. . . .
Oh! poverty, danger and death she can brave,
For the child of her love is no longer a slave.

ETHEL LYNN BEERS (1827–1879)

The famous Civil War poem "All quiet along the Potomac," originally published as "The Picket Guard" in 1861, was first printed in *Harper's Magazine*. Born in Goshen, New York, Ethelinda Eliot began to submit her poems to periodicals under the name Ethel Lynn (adding "Beers" after her marriage in 1846). She often contributed to the *New York Ledger*, and in 1863 published *General Frankie: a Story for Little Folks*. Beers was reluctant to publish her collected poems, sensing that her death would coincide with its publication. Her eerie prediction came true; Beers died on October 11—the day after *All Quiet Along the Potomac and Other Poems* was published in 1879.

"All quiet along the Potomac"

"All quiet along the Potomac," they say,
  "Except now and then a stray picket
Is shot, as he walks on his beat to and fro,
  By a rifleman hid in the thicket.
'T is nothing: a private or two, now and then,
  Will not count in the news of the battle;
Not an officer lost—only one of the men,
  Moaning out, all alone, the death rattle."

All quiet along the Potomac tonight,
  Where the soldiers lie peacefully dreaming;
Their tents in the rays of the clear autumn moon,
  Or the light of the watch-fire, are gleaming.
A tremulous sigh of the gentle night-wind
  Through the forest leaves softly is creeping,
While the stars up above, with their glittering eyes,
  Keep guard, for the army is sleeping.

There's only the sound of the lone sentry's tread
  As he tramps from the rock to the fountain,
And thinks of the two in the low trundle-bed
  Far away in the cot on the mountain.
His musket falls slack; his face, dark and grim,
  Grows gentle with memories tender,
As he mutters a prayer for the children asleep—
  For their mother—may Heaven defend her!

The moon seems to shine just as brightly as then,
  That night, when the love yet unspoken
Leaped up to his lips—when low-murmured vows
  Were pledged to be ever unbroken.
Then drawing his sleeve roughly over his eyes,
  He dashes off tears that are welling,
And gathers his gun closer up to its place
  As if to keep down the heart-swelling.

He passes the fountain, the blasted pine-tree;
  The footstep is lagging and weary;
Yet onward he goes, through the broad belt of light,
  Towards the shade of the forest so dreary.
Hark! was it the night-wind that rustled the leaves?
  Was it moonlight so wondrously flashing?
It looked like a rifle . . . "Ha! Mary, good by!"
  The red life-blood is ebbing and plashing.

All quiet along the Potomac tonight—
  No sound save the rush of the river,
While soft falls the dew on the face of the dead—
  The picket's off duty forever!

ROSE TERRY COOKE (1827–1892)

Rose Terry Cooke, born in Connecticut, attended the Hartford Female Seminary and was graduated at sixteen. Cooke was a teacher and governess in New Jersey before concentrating fully on her writing. Her first story was published in *Graham's Magazine* in 1845. At the height of her popularity, Cooke contributed a leading story for the first issue of the *Atlantic Monthly* at the request of James Russell Lowell. Cooke supported herself financially for most of her life, and married for the first time at the age of forty-six. When her husband had financial troubles, Cooke supported him and her stepchildren by selling her stories to magazines.

Bluebeard's Closet

Fasten the chamber!
Hide the red key;
Cover the portal,
That eyes may not see.
Get thee to market,
To wedding and prayer;
Labor or revel,
The chamber is there!

In comes a stranger—
"Thy pictures how fine,
Titian or Guido,
Whose is the sign?"
Looks he behind them?
Ah! have a care!
"Here is a finer."
The chamber is there!

Fair spreads the banquet,
Rich the array;
See the bright torches
Mimicking day;
When harp and viol
Thrill the soft air,
Comes a light whisper:
The chamber is there!

Marble and painting,
Jasper and gold,
Purple from Tyrus,
Fold upon fold,

Blossoms and jewels,
Thy palace prepare:
Pale grows the monarch;
The chamber is there!

Once it was open
As shore to the sea;
White were the turrets,
Goodly to see;
All through the casements
Flowed the sweet air;
Now it is darkness;
The chamber is there!

Silence and horror
Brood on the walls;
Through every crevice
A little voice calls:
"Quicken, mad footsteps,
On pavement and stair;
Look not behind thee,
The chamber is there!"

Out of the gateway,
Through the wide world,
Into the tempest
Beaten and hurled,
Vain is thy wandering,
Sure thy despair,
Flying or staying,
The chamber is there!

Segovia and Madrid

It sings to me in sunshine,
It whispers all day long,
My heartache like an echo
Repeats the wistful song:
Only a quaint old love-lilt,
Wherein my life is hid,—
"My body is in Segovia,
But my soul is in Madrid!"

I dream, and wake, and wonder,
For dream and day are one,
Alight with vanished faces,
And days forever done.
They smile and shine around me
As long ago they did;
For my body is in Segovia,
But my soul is in Madrid!

Through inland hills and forests
I hear the ocean breeze,
The creak of straining cordage,
The rush of mighty seas,
The lift of angry billows
Through which a swift keel slid;
For my body is in Segovia,
But my soul is in Madrid.

O fair-haired little darlings
Who bore my heart away!
A wide and woful ocean
Between us roars to-day;
Yet am I close beside you
Though time and space forbid;
My body is in Segovia,
But my soul is in Madrid.

If I were once in heaven,
There would be no more sea;
My heart would cease to wander,
My sorrows cease to be;
My sad eyes sleep forever,
In dust and daisies hid,
And my body leave Segovia.
—Would my soul forget Madrid?

HELEN HUNT JACKSON (1830–1885)

Close friends with Emily Dickinson in Amherst, Massachusetts, Helen Hunt Jackson was the daughter of a classics professor. After the death of her husband and her two young sons, the grief-stricken Jackson turned to writing. Using the pseudonyms "Saxe Holm" and "H. H.," she contributed poems to the *New York Evening Post*, the *Nation*, and a few others. Her books of poetry were published in the 1870s, and during this time, Jackson remarried and moved to Colorado. While there, she sympathized with the plight of the Indians, and wrote A *Century of Dishonor* (1881) and *Ramona* (1884), both of which described the cruel treatment of Native Americans. In 1882, Jackson was appointed by the U.S. government to investigate the condition of the Mission Indians of California.

My Lighthouses

At westward window of a palace gray,
Which its own secret still so safely keeps
That no man now its builder's name can say,
I lie and idly sun myself to-day,
Dreaming awake far more than one who sleeps,
Serenely glad, although my gladness weeps.

I look across the harbor's misty blue,
And find and lose that magic shifting line
Where sky one shade less blue meets sea, and through
The air I catch one flush as if it knew
Some secret of that meeting, which no sign
Can show to eyes so far and dim as mine.

More ships than I can count build mast by mast
Gay lattice-work with waving green and red
Across my window-panes. The voyage past,
They crowd to anchorage so glad, so fast,
Gliding like ghosts, with noiseless breath and tread,
Mooring like ghosts, with noiseless iron and lead.

"O ships and patient men who fare by sea,"
I stretch my hands and vainly questioning cry,
"Sailed ye from west? How many nights could ye
Tell by the lights just where my dear and free
And lovely land lay sleeping? Passed ye by
Some danger safe, because her fires were nigh?"

Ah me! my selfish yearning thoughts forget
How darkness but a hand's-breadth from the coast

With danger in an evil league is set!
Ah! helpless ships and men more helpless yet,
Who trust the land-lights' short and empty boast;
The lights ye bear aloft and prayers avail ye most.

But I—ah, patient men who fare by sea,
Ye would but smile to hear this empty speech,—
I have such beacon-lights to burn for me,
In that dear west so lovely, new, and free,
That evil league by day, by night, can teach
No spell whose harm my little bark can reach.

No towers of stone uphold those beacon-lights;
No distance hides them, and no storm can shake;
In valleys they light up the darkest nights,
They outshine sunny days on sunny heights;
They blaze from every house where sleep or wake
My own who love me for my own poor sake.

Each thought they think of me lights road of flame
Across the seas; no travel on it tires
My heart. I go if they but speak my name;
From Heaven I should come and go the same,
And find this glow forestalling my desires.
My darlings, do you hear me? Trim the fires!

Poppies on the Wheat

Along Ancona's hills the shimmering heat,
A tropic tide of air with ebb and flow
Bathes all the fields of wheat until they glow
Like flashing seas of green, which toss and beat
Around the vines. The poppies lithe and fleet
Seem running, fiery torchmen, to and fro
To mark the shore.
                    The farmer does not know
That they are there. He walks with heavy feet,
Counting the bread and wine by autumn's gain,
But I,—I smile to think that days remain
Perhaps to me in which, though bread be sweet
No more, and red wine warm my blood in vain,
I shall be glad remembering how the fleet,
Lithe poppies ran like torchmen with the wheat.

EMILY DICKINSON (1830–1886)

Emily Dickinson, one of the most famous American poets of all time, was born in Amherst, Massachusetts, and educated at Mount Holyoke Female Seminary. Dickinson led a reclusive life, writing her poetry on tiny scraps of paper that she never intended to have published. One of her poems was published anonymously by fellow poet Helen Hunt Jackson, a lifelong friend. Dickinson never married, and hardly ever left her home. Her sister, Lavinia, Mabel Loomis Todd, and Thomas Wentworth Higginson published *Poems by Emily Dickinson* (1890) after her death. This was followed by *Poems: Second Series* (1891) and *Poems: Third Series* (1896). Dickinson left a poetic legacy of over 1,700 lyrical poems that remain popular today.

"Success is counted sweetest"

Success is counted sweetest
By those who ne'er succeed.
To comprehend a nectar
Requires sorest need.

Not one of all the purple host
Who took the flag to-day
Can tell the definition,
So clear, of victory,

As he, defeated, dying,
On whose forbidden ear
The distant strains of triumph
Break, agonized and clear.

"Wild nights! Wild nights!"

Wild nights! Wild nights!
Were I with thee,
Wild nights should be
Our luxury!

Futile the winds
To a heart in port,—
Done with the compass,
Done with the chart.

Rowing in Eden!
Ah! the sea!
Might I but moor
To-night in thee!

"A wounded deer leaps highest"

A wounded deer leaps highest,
I've heard the hunter tell;
'Tis but the ecstasy of death,
And then the brake is still.

The smitten rock that gushes,
The trampled steel that springs:
A cheek is always redder
Just where the hectic stings!

Mirth is the mail of anguish,
In which it cautious arm,
Lest anybody spy the blood
And "You're hurt" exclaim!

"Hope is the thing with feathers"

Hope is the thing with feathers
That perches in the soul,
And sings the tune without the words,
And never stops at all,

And sweetest in the gale is heard;
And sore must be the storm
That could abash the little bird
That kept so many warm.

I've heard it in the chillest land,
And on the strangest sea;
Yet, never, in extremity,
It asked a crumb of me.

"There's a certain slant of light"

There's a certain slant of light,
On winter afternoons,
That oppresses, like the weight
Of cathedral tunes.

Heavenly hurt it gives us;
We can find no scar,
But internal difference
Where the meanings are.

None may teach it anything,
'T is the seal, despair,—
An imperial affliction
Sent us of the air.

When it comes, the landscape listens,
Shadows hold their breath;
When it goes 't is like the distance
On the look of death.

"I felt a funeral in my brain"

I felt a funeral in my brain,
    And mourners, to and fro,
Kept treading, treading, till it seemed
    That sense was breaking through.

And when they all were seated,
    A service like a drum
Kept beating, beating, till I thought
    My mind was going numb.

And then I heard them lift a box,
    And creak across my soul
With those same boots of lead, again.
    Then space began to toll

As all the heavens were a bell,
    And Being but an ear,
And I and silence some strange race,
    Wrecked, solitary, here.

"I'm nobody! Who are you?"

I'm nobody! Who are you?
Are you nobody, too?
Then there's a pair of us—don't tell!
They'd banish us, you know.

How dreary to be somebody!
How public, like a frog
To tell your name the livelong day
To an admiring bog!

"He fumbles at your spirit"

He fumbles at your spirit
   As players at the keys
Before they drop full music on;
   He stuns you by degrees,

Prepares your brittle substance
   For the ethereal blow,
By fainter hammers, further heard,
   Then nearer, then so slow

Your breath has time to straighten,
   Your brain to bubble cool,—
Deals one imperial thunderbolt
   That scalps your naked soul.

"A bird came down the walk"

A bird came down the walk:
He did not know I saw;
He bit an angle-worm in halves
And ate the fellow, raw.

And then he drank a dew
From a convenient grass,
And then hopped sidewise to the wall
To let a beetle pass.

He glanced with rapid eyes
That hurried all abroad,—
They looked like frightened beads, I thought;
He stirred his velvet head

Like one in danger; cautious,
I offered him a crumb,
And he unrolled his feathers
And rowed him softer home

Than oars divide the ocean,
Too silver for a seam,
Or butterflies, off banks of noon,
Leap, plashless, as they swim.

"This is my letter to the world"

This is my letter to the world,
   That never wrote to me,—
The simple news that Nature told,
   With tender majesty.

Her message is committed
   To hands I cannot see;
For love of her, sweet countrymen,
   Judge tenderly of me!

"I heard a fly buzz when I died"

I heard a fly buzz when I died;
   The stillness round my form
Was like the stillness in the air
   Between the heaves of storm.

The eyes beside had wrung them dry,
   And breaths were gathering sure
For that last onset, when the king
   Be witnessed in his power.

I willed my keepsakes, signed away
   What portion of me I
Could make assignable,—and then
   There interposed a fly,

With blue, uncertain, stumbling buzz,
   Between the light and me;
And then the windows failed, and then
   I could not see to see.

"Because I could not stop for Death"

Because I could not stop for Death,
He kindly stopped for me;
The carriage held but just ourselves
And Immortality.

We slowly drove, he knew no haste,
And I had put away

My labor, and my leisure too,
For his civility.

We passed the school where children played,
Their lessons scarcely done;
We passed the fields of gazing grain,
We passed the setting sun.

We paused before a house that seemed
A swelling of the ground;
The roof was scarcely visible,
The cornice but a mound.

Since then 't is centuries; but each
Feels shorter than the day
I first surmised the horses' heads
Were toward eternity.

"If I can stop one heart from breaking"

If I can stop one heart from breaking,
I shall not live in vain;
If I can ease one life the aching,
Or cool one pain,
Or help one fainting robin
Unto his nest again,
I shall not live in vain.

"A narrow fellow in the grass"

A narrow fellow in the grass
Occasionally rides;
You may have met him,—did you not,
His notice sudden is.

The grass divides as with a comb,
A spotted shaft is seen;
And then it closes at your feet
And opens further on.

He likes a boggy acre,
A floor too cool for corn.
Yet when a child, and barefoot,
I more than once, at morn,

Have passed, I thought, a whip-lash
Unbraiding in the sun, —
When, stooping to secure it,
It wrinkled, and was gone.

Several of nature's people
I know, and they know me;
I feel for them a transport
Of cordiality;

But never met this fellow,
Attended or alone,
Without a tighter breathing,
And zero at the bone.

"I never saw a moor"

I never saw a moor,
I never saw the sea;
Yet know I how the heather looks,
And what a wave must be.

I never spoke with God,
Nor visited in heaven;
Yet certain am I of the spot
As if the chart were given.

"There is no frigate like a book"

There is no frigate like a book
    To take us lands away,
Nor any coursers like a page
    Of prancing poetry.
This traverse may the poorest take
    Without oppress of toll;
How frugal is the chariot
    That bears a human soul!

"My life closed twice before its close"

My life closed twice before its close;
    It yet remains to see
If Immortality unveil
    A third event to me,

So huge, so hopeless to conceive,
    As these that twice befell.
Parting is all we know of heaven,
    And all we need of hell.

NORA PERRY (1831–1896)

Nora Perry, born in Dudley, Massachusetts, and raised in Providence, Rhode Island, had her first short story published in *Harper's Magazine* when she was eighteen. She worked as a Boston correspondent for the *Chicago Tribune* and the *Providence Journal*. One of her best known poems, "The Love-Knot," originally published in the *National Era*, is included here. Perry wrote poetry, novels, and stories for girls, including *After the Ball, and Other Poems* (1875), *Her Lover's Friend, and Other Poems* (1880), *For a Woman, a novel* (1885), and *Hope Benham, a Story for Girls* (1894).

The Love-Knot

Tying her bonnet under her chin,
She tied her raven ringlets in;
But not alone in the silken snare
Did she catch her lovely floating hair,
For, tying her bonnet under her chin,
She tied a young man's heart within.

They were strolling together up the hill,
Where the wind comes blowing merry and chill;
And it blew the curls, a frolicsome race,
All over the happy peach-colored face,
Till, scolding and laughing, she tied them in,
Under her beautiful dimpled chin.

And it blew a color, bright as the bloom
Of the pinkest fuchsia's tossing plume,
All over the cheeks of the prettiest girl
That ever imprisoned a romping curl,
Or, tying her bonnet under her chin,
Tied a young man's heart within.

Steeper and steeper grew the hill;
Madder, merrier, chillier still
The western wind blew down, and played
The wildest tricks with the little maid,
As, tying her bonnet under her chin,
She tied a young man's heart within.

O western wind, do you think it was fair
To play such tricks with her floating hair!
To gladly, gleefully do your best

To blow her against the young man's breast,
Where he as gladly folded her in,
And kissed her mouth and her dimpled chin?

Ah! Ellery Vane, you little thought,
An hour ago, when you besought
This country lass to walk with you,
After the sun had dried the dew,
What perilous danger you'd be in,
As she tied her bonnet under her chin!

LOUISA MAY ALCOTT (1832–1888)

Born in Germantown, Pennsylvania, Louisa May Alcott was educated by her father, Bronson Alcott. She began to write for publication at the age of sixteen. Her first book, *Flower Fables*, was published when she was twenty-two. Her poems and short stories were often printed in the *Atlantic Monthly*. Much of Alcott's work was autobiographical; her job as a volunteer nurse in the Union Hospital during the Civil War resulted in *Hospital Sketches* (1863). Alcott's fame is centered on her novel *Little Women* (1868), which tells of her own family life. The book became tremendously popular, and started a series of sequels, among them *Little Men* (1871) and *Jo's Boys* (1886). Alcott supported both women's suffrage and the temperance movement.

Thoreau's Flute

We, sighing, said, "Our Pan is dead;
   His pipe hangs mute beside the river;
   Around it wistful sunbeams quiver,
But Music's airy voice is fled.
Spring mourns as for untimely frost;
   The bluebird chants a requiem;
   The willow-blossom waits for him;—
The Genius of the wood is lost."

Then from the flute, untouched by hands,
   There came a low, harmonious breath:
   "For such as he there is no death;
His life the eternal life commands;
Above man's aims his nature rose:
   The wisdom of a just content
   Made one small spot a continent,
And turned to poetry Life's prose.

"Haunting the hills, the stream, the wild,
   Swallow and aster, lake and pine,
   To him grew human or divine,—
Fit mates for this large-hearted child.
Such homage Nature ne'er forgets,
   And yearly on the coverlid
   'Neath which her darling lieth hid
Will write his name in violets.

"To him no vain regrets belong,
   Whose soul, that finer instrument,
   Gave to the world no poor lament,
But wood-notes ever sweet and strong.
O lonely friend! he still will be
   A potent presence, though unseen,—
   Steadfast, sagacious, and serene:
Seek not for him,—he is with thee."

MARY ASHLEY TOWNSEND (1832–1901)

Using the pseudonym "Xariffa," Mary Ashley Townsend contributed a series of essays entitled "Quillotypes" to the New Orleans *Delta*. She also published articles in the *Crescent* under the name "Mary Ashley" and sent in letters about her trip to Mexico. Her first book was a novel, and was followed by *Xariffa's Poems* (1870). *The Captain's Story* (1874), a dramatic verse about a white man who discovers his mother was biracial, was highly praised by Oliver Wendell Holmes. *Down the Bayou and Other Poems* (1881) contained "Creed," her most well-known poem at the time. Married with three daughters, Townsend was chosen to write for the New Orleans Cotton Exposition, and was the first American woman to be a member of the Liceo Hidalgo, a literary club in Mexico.

Creed

I believe if I should die,
And you should kiss my eyelids when I lie
  Cold, dead, and dumb to all the world contains,
The folded orbs would open at thy breath,
And, from its exile in the isles of death,
  Life would come gladly back along my veins.

I believe if I were dead,
And you upon my lifeless heart should tread,
  Not knowing what the poor clod chanced to be,
It would find sudden pulse beneath the touch
Of him it ever loved in life so much,
  And throb again, warm, tender, true to thee.

I believe if on my grave,
Hidden in woody deeps or by the wave,
  Your eyes should drop some warm tears of regret,
From every salty seed of your dear grief,
Some fair, sweet blossom would leap into leaf,
  To prove death could not make my love forget.

I believe if I should fade
Into those mystic realms where light is made,
  And you should long once more my face to see,
I would come forth upon the hills of night
And gather stars, like fagots, till thy sight,
  Led by their beacon blaze, fell full on me!

I believe my faith in thee,
Strong as my life, so nobly placed to be,
    I would as soon expect to see the sun
Fall like a dead king from his height sublime,
His glory stricken from the throne of time,
        As thee unworth the worship thou hast won.

I believe who hath not loved
Hath half the sweetness of his life unproved;
    Like one who, with the grape within his grasp,
Drops it with all its crimson juice unpressed,
And all its luscious sweetness left unguessed,
        Out from his careless and unheeding clasp.

I believe love, pure and true,
Is to the soul a sweet, immortal dew,
    That gems life's petals in its hours of dusk;
The waiting angels see and recognize
The rich crown jewel, Love, of Paradise,
        When life falls from us like a withered husk.

Virtuosa

As by the instrument she took her place,
The expectant people, breathing sigh nor word,
Sat hushed, while o'er the waiting ivory stirred
Her supple hands with their suggestive grace.
With sweet notes they began to interlace,
And then with lofty strains their skill to gird,
Then loftier still, till all the echoes heard
Entrancing harmonies float into space.
She paused, and gaily trifled with the keys
Until they laughed in wild delirium,
Then, with rebuking fingers, from their glees
She led them one by one till all grew dumb,
And music seemed to sink upon its knees,
A slave her touch could quicken or benumb.

Her Horoscope

'T is true, one half of woman's life is hope
And one half resignation. Between there lies
Anguish of broken dreams,—doubt, dire surprise,
And then is born the strength with all to cope.

Unconsciously sublime, life's shadowed slope
She braves; the knowledge in her patient eyes
Of all that love bestows and love denies,
As writ in every woman's horoscope!
She lives, her heart-beats given to others' needs,
Her hands, to lift for others on the way
The burdens which their weariness forsook.
She dies, an uncrowned doer of great deeds.
Remembered? Yes, as is for one brief day
The rose one leaves in some forgotten book.

A Georgia Volunteer

Far up the lonely mountain-side
    My wandering footsteps led;
The moss lay thick beneath my feet,
    The pine sighed overhead.
The trace of a dismantled fort
    Lay in the forest nave,
And in the shadow near my path
    I saw a soldier's grave.

The bramble wrestled with the weed
    Upon the lowly mound; —
The simple head-board, rudely writ,
    Had rotted to the ground;
I raised it with a reverent hand,
    From dust its words to clear,
But time had blotted all but these —
    "A Georgia Volunteer!"

I saw the toad and scaly snake
    From tangled covert start,
And hide themselves among the weeds
    Above the dead man's heart;
But undisturbed, in sleep profound,
    Unheeding, there he lay;
His coffin but the mountain soil,
    His shroud Confederate gray.

I heard the Shenandoah roll
    Along the vale below,
I saw the Alleghanies rise
    Towards the realms of snow.

The "Valley Campaign" rose to mind—
    Its leader's name—and then
I knew the sleeper had been one
    Of Stonewall Jackson's men.

Yet whence he came, what lip shall say—
    Whose tongue will ever tell
What desolated hearths and hearts
    Have been because he fell?
What sad-eyed maiden braids her hair,
    Her hair which he held dear?
One lock of which perchance lies with
    The Georgia Volunteer!

What mother, with long watching eyes,
    And white lips cold and dumb,
Waits with appalling patience for
    Her darling boy to come?
Her boy! whose mountain grave swells up
    But one of many a scar,
Cut on the face of our fair land,
    By gory-handed war.

What fights he fought, what wounds he wore,
    Are all unknown to fame;
Remember, on his lonely grave
    There is not e'en a name!
That he fought well and bravely too,
    And held his country dear,
We know, else he had never been
    A Georgia Volunteer.

He sleeps—what need to question now
    If he were wrong or right?
He knows, ere this, whose cause was just
    In God the Father's sight.
He wields no warlike weapons now,
    Returns no foeman's thrust—
Who but a coward would revile
    An honest soldier's dust?

Roll, Shenandoah, proudly roll,
  Adown thy rocky glen,
Above thee lies the grave of one
  Of Stonewall Jackson's men.
Beneath the cedar and the pine,
  In solitude austere,
Unknown, unnamed, forgotten, lies
  A Georgia Volunteer.

ELIZABETH AKERS ALLEN (1832–1911)

Elizabeth Akers Allen grew up in Farmington, Maine. Her first book of poems, under the pseudonym "Florence Percy," was published in 1856. After the success of this first volume of poems, Allen traveled to Europe and worked as a correspondent for the Portland *Transcript* and the *Boston Evening Gazette*. While in Rome, Allen met a Maine sculptor who would become her second husband. (Her first marriage was brief, ending in divorce.) In 1865, she married for the third time and the two made their home in Virginia and Maine before settling in Tuckahoe, New York, after 1881. Meanwhile, Allen worked as a government clerk in Washington, D.C., and as literary editor for the Portland *Daily Advertiser*. Her best-known work, the poem "Rock Me to Sleep," was first published in the *Saturday Evening Post* in 1860.

Rock Me to Sleep

Backward, turn backward, O Time, in your flight,
Make me a child again just for to-night!
Mother, come back from the echoless shore,
Take me again to your heart as of yore;
Kiss from my forehead the furrows of care,
Smooth the few silver threads out of my hair;
Over my slumbers your loving watch keep;—
Rock me to sleep, mother—rock me to sleep!

Backward, flow backward, O tide of the years!
I am so weary of toil and of tears,—
Toil without recompense, tears all in vain,—
Take them, and give me my childhood again!
I have grown weary of dust and decay,—
Weary of flinging my soul-wealth away;
Weary of sowing for others to reap;—
Rock me to sleep, mother,—rock me to sleep!

Tired of the hollow, the base, the untrue,
Mother, O mother, my heart calls for you!
Many a summer the grass has grown green,
Blossomed and faded, our faces between:
Yet, with strong yearning and passionate pain,
Long I to-night for your presence again.
Come from the silence so long and so deep;—
Rock me to sleep, mother,—rock me to sleep!

Over my heart, in the days that are flown,
No love like mother-love ever has shone;

No other worship abides and endures,—
Faithful, unselfish, and patient like yours:
None like a mother can charm away pain
From the sick soul and the world-weary brain.
Slumber's soft calms o'er my heavy lids creep;—
Rock me to sleep, mother,—rock me to sleep!

Come, let your brown hair, just lighted with gold,
Fall on your shoulders again as of old;
Let it drop over my forehead to-night,
Shading my faint eyes away from the light;
For with its sunny-edged shadows once more
Haply will throng the sweet visions of yore;
Lovingly, softly, its bright billows sweep;—
Rock me to sleep, mother,—rock me to sleep!

Mother, dear mother, the years have been long
Since I last listened your lullaby song:
Sing, then, and unto my soul it shall seem
Womanhood's years have been only a dream.
Clasped to your heart in a loving embrace,
With your light lashes just sweeping my face,
Never hereafter to wake or to weep;—
Rock me to sleep, mother,—rock me to sleep!

CELIA THAXTER (1835–1894)

Celia Thaxter was born in Portsmouth, New Hampshire, and grew up on Appledore Island in the Isles of Shoals, where her father worked as a lighthouse keeper and owned a summer hotel. Thaxter adored the sea and missed it enormously when she moved to Massachusetts after her marriage in 1851. Homesick for the sea, Thaxter wrote a poem about nature, which was published without her knowledge by James Russell Lowell in the *Atlantic Monthly*. After this, she sent in her poems, children's stories, and sketches for publication in various magazines. Among her books are *Poems* (1872), *Poems for Children* (1884), and the prose *Among the Isles of Shoals* (1886). Thaxter also painted illustrations for her books.

Seaward

To —

How long it seems since that mild April night,
    When, leaning from the window, you and I
Heard, clearly ringing from the shadowy bight,
    The loon's unearthly cry!

Southwest the wind blew, million little waves
    Ran rippling round the point in mellow tune,
But mournful, like the voice of one who raves,
    That laughter of the loon!

We called to him, while blindly through the haze
    Uprose the meagre moon behind us, slow,
So dim, the fleet of boats we scarce could trace,
    Moored lightly just below.

We called, and, lo, he answered! Half in fear
    We sent the note back. Echoing rock and bay
Made melancholy music far and near;
    Sadly it died away.

That schooner, you remember? Flying ghost!
    Her canvas catching every wandering beam,
Aerial, noiseless, past the glimmering coast
    She glided like a dream.

Would we were leaning from your window now,
    Together calling to the eerie loon,
The fresh wind blowing care from either brow,
    This sumptuous night of June!

So many sighs load this sweet inland air,
  'T is hard to breathe, nor can we find relief:
However lightly touched, we all must share
  This nobleness of grief.

But sighs are spent before they reach your ear;
  Vaguely they mingle with the water's rune;
No sadder sound salutes you than the clear,
  Wild laughter of the loon.

The Sandpiper

Across the narrow beach we flit,
  One little sandpiper and I,
And fast I gather, bit by bit,
  The scattered driftwood bleached and dry.
The wild waves reach their hands for it,
  The wild wind raves, the tide runs high,
As up and down the beach we flit,—
  One little sandpiper and I.

Above our heads the sullen clouds
  Scud black and swift across the sky;
Like silent ghosts in misty shrouds
  Stand out the white lighthouses high.
Almost as far as eye can reach
  I see the close-reefed vessels fly,
As fast we flit along the beach,—
  One little sandpiper and I.

I watch him as he skims along,
  Uttering his sweet and mournful cry.
He starts not at my fitful song,
  Or flash of fluttering drapery.
He has no thought of any wrong;
  He scans me with a fearless eye:
Staunch friends are we, well tried and strong,
  The little sandpiper and I.

Comrade, where wilt thou be to-night
  When the loosed storm breaks furiously?
My driftwood fire will burn so bright!
  To what warm shelter canst thou fly?

I do not fear for thee, though wroth
   The tempest rushes through the sky:
For are we not God's children both,
   Thou, little sandpiper, and I?

LOUISE CHANDLER MOULTON (1835–1908)

Louise Chandler Moulton was educated in Pomfret, Connecticut, and spent a year in Emma Hart Willard's Female Seminary in Troy, New York. In 1854, Moulton published the successful book of verse *This, That, and the Other*. A year later, she married a journalist and continued publishing her poems in popular magazines of her day. Her writing was collected in several books such as *Bed-Time Stories* (1874–1880), *Some Women's Hearts* (1874), *Random Rambles* (1881), and a social narrative entitled *Ourselves and Our Neighbors: Short Chats on Social Topics* (1887). In the 1870s and 1880s, Moulton worked as literary correspondent in Boston for the *New York Tribune* and as book critic for the *Boston Sunday Herald*. Living in London after 1876, Moulton befriended several late-Romantic British poets and helped introduce their poetry to America.

To-Night

Bend low, O dusky Night,
   And give my spirit rest.
   Hold me to your deep breast,
And put old cares to flight.
Give back the lost delight
   That once my soul possest,
   When Love was loveliest.
Bend low, O dusky Night!

Enfold me in your arms—
   The sole embrace I crave
   Until the embracing grave
Shield me from life's alarms.
I dare your subtlest charms;
   Your deepest spell I brave,—
   O, strong to slay or save,
Enfold me in your arms!

Louisa May Alcott

In Memoriam

As the wind at play with a spark
   Of fire that glows through the night,
As the speed of the soaring lark
   That wings to the sky his flight,
So swiftly thy soul has sped
   On its upward, wonderful way,

Like the lark, when the dawn is red,
 In search of the shining day.

Thou art not with the frozen dead
 Whom earth in the earth we lay,
While the bearers softly tread,
 And the mourners kneel and pray;
From thy semblance, dumb and stark,
 The soul has taken its flight—
Out of the finite dark,
 Into the Infinite Light.

A Painted Fan

Roses and butterflies snared on a fan,
 All that is left of a summer gone by;
Of swift, bright wings that flashed in the sun,
 And loveliest blossoms that bloomed to die!

By what subtle spell did you lure them here,
 Fixing a beauty that will not change,—
Roses whose petals never will fall,
 Bright, swift wings that never will range?

Had you owned but the skill to snare as well
 The swift-winged hours that came and went,
To prison the words that in music died,
 And fix with a spell the heart's content,

Then had you been of magicians the chief;
 And loved and lovers should bless your art,
If you could but have painted the soul of the thing,—
 Not the rose alone, but the rose's heart!

Flown are those days with their winged delights,
 As the odor is gone from the summer rose;
Yet still, whenever I wave my fan,
 The soft, south wind of memory blows.

AUGUSTA COOPER BRISTOL (1835–1910)

The New Hampshire-born Augusta Cooper Bristol was an educator and lecturer. The youngest of ten children, Bristol excelled in mathematics and reasoning, and wrote poems as a child. She began teaching when she was fifteen years old, and her first marriage, ending in divorce, lasted only five years. She remarried in 1866 and moved to Vineland, New Jersey, with her new husband. Bristol lectured on behalf of numerous societies and traveled extensively as a speaker. She wrote several books on social topics, and her book of poems, *The Web of Life*, was published in 1895.

Night

I stood and watched the still, mysterious Night,
Steal from her shadowy caverns in the East,
To work her deep enchantments on the world.
Her black veil floated down the silent glens,
While her dark sandalled feet, with noiseless tread,
Moved to a secret harmony. Along
The brows of the majestic hills, she strung
Her glorious diamonds so stealthily,
It never marred their dreams; and in the deep,
Cool thickets of the wood, where scarce the Day
Could reach the dim retreat, her dusky hand
Pinned on the breast of the exhaling flower,
A glittering gem; while all the tangled ferns
And forest lace-work, as she moved along,
Grew moist and shining.

                Who would e'er have guessed,
The queenly Night would deign to stoop and love
A little flower! And yet, with all her stealth,
I saw her press her damp and cooling lip
Upon the feverish bosom of a Rose;
At which a watchful bird poured sudden forth
A love-sick song, of sweet and saddest strain.

Upon the ivied rocks, and rugged crags
On which the ocean billows break, she hung
Her sombre mantle; and the gray old sea
That had been high in tumult all the day,
Became so mesmerized beneath her wiles,
He seemed a mere reflection of herself.
The billows sank into a dimpled sleep;

Only the little tide-waves glided up
To kiss the blackness of the airy robe
That floated o'er them.

              Long I stood and watched
The mystic, spell-like influence of Night;
Till o'er the eastern hills, came up the first
Faint glories of the crown that Phœbus wears.
And soon, the Earth, surprised to see the work
That Night had wrought, began to glow and blush,
Like maidens, conscious of the glance of Love.
While she,—the dark Enchantress,—like to one
Who decorates her bower with all things fair,
Wherewith to please her lover, but yet flees
At his approaching step,—at the first gleam
That lit the zenith from the Day-god's eye,
Fled timid o'er the distant western hills.

The Crime of the Ages

1861

      Poet, write!
Not of a purpose dark and dire,
That souls of evil fashion,
Nor the power that nerves the assassin's hand,
In the white heat of his passion:
      But let thy rhyme,
      Through every clime,
A burthen bear of this one crime:
Let the world draw in a shuddering breath,
O'er the crime that aims at a nation's death!

      Minstrel, sing!
Not in affection's dulcet tone,
Or with sound of a soft recorder:
Strike not thy harp to a strain arranged
In measured, harmonic order:
      But loud and strong
      The tones prolong,
That thunder of a Nation's wrong;
Let a sound of war in thy notes appear,
Till the world opes wide a startled ear!

Soldier, fight!
Thou hast a patriot's throbbing pulse,
And future history's pages,
Shall tell of the blood so freely shed
To redeem "the crime of the ages."
Well may'st thou fight
For Truth and Right,
And teach a rebel foe thy might!
Let a loyal heart, and undaunted will,
Show the world we are a Nation still!

Prophet, speak!
Speak for the children of martyred sires,
An offspring the most ungrateful!
Warn them of Justice hurrying on,
To punish a deed so hateful!
O read with thy
Prophetic eye,
The omens of our troubled sky!
What is the picture beyond the gloom?
New life, new birth, or a Nation's tomb?

SARAH MORGAN PIATT (1836–1919)

Sarah Morgan Piatt's family was one of the earliest settlers of the state of Kentucky. After her mother's death, eight-year-old Piatt and her younger sister went to live with an aunt in New Castle, where they were educated. Piatt was an avid reader and enjoyed the works of Shelley, Coleridge, Byron, and Hemans. Her early verses were published in the *Louisville Journal* and the *New York Ledger*. In 1861, Piatt married and moved with her husband to Washington, D.C. Her numerous volumes of poems include: *The Nests at Washington, and Other Poems* (1864), *A Woman's Poems* (1871), and *A Voyage to the Fortunate Isles* (1874). In 1882, Piatt moved to Ireland, where her husband was U.S. consul. While there, she wrote of her experiences, publishing *An Irish Garland* (1884) and *An Irish Wild-Flower* (1891).

Giving Back the Flower

So, because you chose to follow me into the subtle sadness of night,
   And to stand in the half-set moon with the weird fall-light on your
      glimmering hair,
Till your presence hid all of the earth and all of the sky from my sight,
   And to give me a little scarlet bud, that was dying of frost, to wear,

Say, must you taunt me forever, forever? You looked at my hand and
     you knew
   That I was the slave of the Ring, while you were as free as the wind
      is free.
When I saw your corpse in your coffin, I flung back your flower to you;
   It was all of yours that I ever had; you must keep it, and—keep from
      me.

Ah? so God is your witness. Has God, then, no world to look after but
     ours?
   May He not have been searching for that wild star, with the trailing
      plumage, that flew
Far over a part of our darkness while we were there by the freezing
     flowers,
   Or else brightening some planet's luminous rings, instead of think-
      ing of you?

Or, if He was near us at all, do you think that He would sit listening
     there
   Because you sang "Hear me, Norma," to a woman in jewels and
      lace,
While, so close to us, down in another street, in the wet, unlighted air,
   There were children crying for bread and fire, and mothers who
      questioned His grace?

Or perhaps He had gone to the ghastly field where the fight had been
    that day,
  To number the bloody stabs that were there, to look at and judge the
    dead;
Or else to the place full of fever and moans where the wretched
    wounded lay;
  At least I do not believe that He cares to remember a word that you
    said.

So take back your flower, I tell you—of its sweetness I now have no
    need;
  Yes, take back your flower down into the stillness and mystery to
    keep;
When you wake I will take it, and God, then, perhaps will witness in-
    deed,
  But go, now, and tell Death he must watch you, and not let you walk
    in your sleep.

My Babes in the Wood

I know a story, fairer, dimmer, sadder,
    Than any story painted in your books.
You are so glad? It will not make you gladder;
    Yet listen, with your pretty restless looks.

"Is it a Fairy Story?" Well, half fairy—
    At least it dates far back as fairies do,
And seems to me as beautiful and airy;
    Yet half, perhaps the fairy half, is true.

You had a baby sister and a brother,
    (Two very dainty people, rosily white,
Each sweeter than all things except the other!)
    Older yet younger—gone from human sight!

And I, who loved them, and shall love them ever,
    And think with yearning tears how each light hand
Crept toward bright bloom or berries—I shall never
    Know how I lost them. Do you understand?

Poor slightly golden heads! I think I missed them
    First, in some dreamy, piteous, doubtful way;
But when and where with lingering lips I kissed them,
    My gradual parting, I can never say.

Sometimes I fancy that they may have perished
  In shadowy quiet of wet rocks and moss,
Near paths whose very pebbles I have cherished,
  For their small sakes, since my most lovely loss.

I fancy, too, that they were softly covered
  By robins, out of apple-flowers they knew,
Whose nursing wings in far home sunshine hovered,
  Before the timid world had dropped the dew.

Their names were—what yours are! At this you wonder.
  Their pictures are—your own, as you have seen;
And my bird-buried darlings, hidden under
  Lost leaves—why, it is your dead selves I mean!

Transfigured

Almost afraid they led her in
  (A dwarf more piteous none could find):
Withered as some weird leaf, and thin,
  The woman was—and wan and blind.

Into his mirror with a smile—
  Not vain to be so fair, but glad—
The South-born painter looked the while,
  With eyes than Christ's alone less sad.

"Mother of God," in pale surprise
  He whispered, "what am I to paint!"
A voice, that sounded from the skies,
  Said to him, "Raphael, a saint."

She sat before him in the sun:
  He scarce could look at her, and she
Was still and silent. . . . "It is done,"
  He said.—"Oh, call the world to see!"

Ah, this was she is veriest truth—
  Transcendent face and haloed hair.
The beauty of divinest youth,
  Divinely beautiful, was there.

Herself into her picture passed—
  Herself and not her poor disguise,
Made up of time and dust. . . . At last
  One saw her with the Master's eyes.

CHARLOTTE L. FORTEN GRIMKÉ (1837–1914)

Charlotte L. Forten Grimké, born into a wealthy African-American family in Philadelphia, published one of the earliest journal accounts of an African-American woman. *The Journal of Charlotte L. Forten* (1953), written between 1854 and 1864, focuses on African-American life and discrimination in nine-teenth-century America. Grimké became the first black to teach white children in Salem, Massachusetts, in 1856. An antislavery advocate, Grimké volunteered at a school for ex-slaves and their children, writing *Life on the Sea Islands* (published in the *Atlantic Monthly* in 1864) about her experiences there. Her poems, written under her maiden name and under pseudonyms "Miss C. L. F." and "Lottie," were published in abolitionist periodicals of the time such as the *Liberator, The Dunbar Speaker and Entertainer,* and the *National Anti-Slavery Standard.*

Poem

In the earnest path of duty,
　　With the high hopes and hearts sincere,
We, to useful lives aspiring,
　　Daily meet to labor here.

No vain dreams of earthly glory
　　Urge us onward to explore
Far-extending realms of knowledge,
　　With their rich and varied store;

But, with hope of aiding others,
　　Gladly we perform our part;
Nor forget, the mind, while storing,
　　We must educate the heart,—

Teach it hatred of oppression,
　　Truest love of God and man;
Thus our high and holy calling
　　May accomplish His great plan.

Not the great and gifted only
　　He appoints to do his will,
But each one, however lowly,
　　Has a mission to fulfill.

Knowing this, toil we unwearied,
　　With true hearts and purpose high;—
We would win a wreath immortal
　　Whose bright flowers ne'er fade and die.

A Parting Hymn

When Winter's royal robes of white
From hill and vale are gone
And the glad voices of the spring
Upon the air are borne,
Friends who have met with us before,
Within these walls shall meet no more.

Forth to a noble work they go:
O, may their hearts keep pure,
And hopeful zeal and strength be theirs
To labor and endure,
That they an earnest faith may prove
By words of truth and deeds of love.

May those, whose holy task it is,
To guide impulsive youth,
Fail not to cherish in their souls
A reverence for truth;
For teachings which the lips impart
Must have their source within the heart.

May all who suffer share their love—
The poor and the oppressed;
So shall the blessing of our God
Upon their labors rest.
And may we meet again where all
Are blest and freed from every thrall.

MARY MAPES DODGE (1838–1905)

Educated by private tutors in New York City, Mary Mapes Dodge got her start in writing at her father's magazine in 1847. With two children to support, the newly widowed Dodge began writing stories for publication in juvenile magazines, and her first book appeared in 1864. She wrote the children's classic *Hans Brinker; or The Silver Skates* (1865), which included detailed descriptions of Dutch life and customs. *Hans Brinker* was a great success, and was translated into many foreign languages. In 1868, she became associate editor of *Hearth and Home* with Harriet Beecher Stowe and Donald G. Mitchell. Named editor of *St. Nicholas Magazine* for children, Dodge secured high standards for its writing and artwork. She died in her summer home in Onteora Park, New York, in 1905.

The Minuet

Grandma told me all about it,
Told me so I couldn't doubt it,
How she danced, my grandma danced; long ago
How she held her pretty head,
How her dainty skirt she spread,
How she slowly leaned and rose—long ago.

Grandma's hair was bright and sunny,
Dimpled cheeks, too, oh, how funny!
Really quite a pretty girl—long ago.
Bless her! why, she wears a cap,
Grandma does, and takes a nap
Every single day: and yet
Grandma danced the minuet—long ago.

"Modern ways are quite alarming,"
Grandma says, "but boys were charming"
(Girls and boys she means, of course) "long ago."
Brave but modest, grandly shy;
She would like to have us try
Just to feel like those who met
In the graceful minuet—long ago.

Now the Noisy Winds Are Still

Now the noisy winds are still;
April's coming up the hill!
All the spring is in her train,
Led by shining ranks of rain;
   Pit, pat, patter, clatter,
   Sudden sun, and clatter, patter!—
First the blue, and then the shower;
Bursting bud, and smiling flower;
Brooks set free with tinkling ring;
Birds too full of song to sing;
Crisp old leaves astir with pride,
Where the timid violets hide—
All things ready with a will—
April's coming up the hill!

Emerson

We took it to the woods, we two,
   The book well worn and brown,
To read his words where stirring leaves
   Rained their soft shadows down.

Yet as we sat and breathed the scene,
   We opened not a page;
Enough that he was with us there,
   Our silent, friendly sage!

His fresh "Rhodora" bloomed again;
   His "Humble-bee" buzzed near;
And oh, the "Wood-notes" beautiful
   He taught our souls to hear.

So our unopened book was read;
   And so, in restful mood,
We and our poet, arm in arm,
   Went sauntering through the wood.

MARGARET E. SANGSTER (1838–1912)

Margaret E. Sangster learned to read at the age of four and studied Latin, Greek, and French. In 1855, she sold a children's story, *Little Janey*, for forty dollars to the Presbyterian Board of Publication, which then gave her a commission to write a hundred more stories. After her husband's death in 1871, Sangster assumed the editorship of the children's page of *Hearth and Home* from Mary Mapes Dodge. Her pious and practical writings were highly valued, and she contributed many letters and essays to the periodicals of her time. Sangster became an editor for the *Christian Intelligencer* in 1876, a literary advisor to Harper & Brothers, and edited *Harper's Bazar* (1889–99). She also published several novels, collections of verse, and an autobiography in 1909.

A Song for Our Flag

A bit of color against the blue:
Hues of the morning, blue for true,
And red for the kindling light of flame,
And white for a nation's stainless fame.
Oh! fling it forth to the winds afar,
With hope in its every shining star:
Under its folds wherever found,
Thank God, we have freedom's holy ground.

Don't you love it, as out it floats
From the school house peak, and glad young throats
Sing of the banner that aye shall be
Symbol of honor and victory?
Don't you thrill when the marching feet
Of jubilant soldiers shake the street,
And the bugles shrill, and the trumpets call,
And the red, white, and blue is over us all?
Don't you pray, amid starting tears,
It may never be furled through age-long years?

A song for our flag, our country's boast,
That gathers beneath it a mighty host;
Long may it wave o'er the goodly land
We hold in fee 'neath our Father's hand.
For God and liberty evermore
May that banner stand from shore to shore,
Never to those high meanings lost,
Never with alien standards crossed,
But always valiant and pure and true,
Our starry flag: red, white, and blue.

CONSTANCE FENIMORE WOOLSON (1840–1894)

Constance Fenimore Woolson, a great-niece of author James Fenimore Cooper, was born in New Hampshire. Woolson's family moved to Cleveland, Ohio, after her three sisters died of scarlet fever. After her father's death in 1869, Woolson traveled with her mother to the South while contributing sketches to magazines. Her first book, *The Old Stone House* (1872), was published under the pseudonym "Anne March." Woolson's stories began to reflect her travels, and in 1879 she settled in Europe. Her novels were originally published serially in *Harper's* before appearing in book form as *Anne* (1882) and *For the Major* (1883). Woolson also published short story collections, verse, and travel sketches. Suffering from depression, she died in 1894 after falling from a window in her Venice apartment.

Love Unexpressed

The sweetest notes among the human heart-strings
    Are dull with rust;
The sweetest chords, adjusted by the angels,
    Are clogged with dust;
We pipe and pipe again our dreary music
    Upon the self-same strains,
While sounds of crime, and fear, and desolation,
    Come back in sad refrains.

On through the world we go, an army marching
    With listening ears,
Each longing, sighing, for the heavenly music
    He never hears;
Each longing, sighing, for a word of comfort,
    A word of tender praise,
A word of love, to cheer the endless journey
    Of earth's hard, busy days.

They love us, and we know it; this suffices
    For reason's share.
Why should they pause to give that love expression
    With gentle care?
Why should they pause? But still our hearts are aching
    With all the gnawing pain
Of hungry love that longs to hear the music,
    And longs and longs in vain.

We love them, and they know it; if we falter,
   With fingers numb,
Among the unused strings of love's expression,
   The notes are dumb.
We shrink within ourselves in voiceless sorrow,
   Leaving the words unsaid,
And, side by side with those we love the dearest,
   In silence on we tread.

Thus on we tread, and thus each heart in silence
   Its fate fulfils,
Waiting and hoping for the heavenly music
   Beyond the distant hills.
The only difference of the love in heaven
   From love on earth below
Is: Here we love and know not how to tell it,
   And there we all shall know.

Yellow Jessamine

In tangled wreaths, in clustered gleaming stars,
   In floating, curling sprays,
The golden flower comes shining through the woods
   These February days;
Forth go all hearts, all hands, from out the town,
   To bring her gayly in,
This wild, sweet Princess of far Florida—
   The yellow jessamine.

The live-oaks smile to see her lovely face
   Peep from the thickets; shy,
She hides behind the leaves her golden buds
   Till, bolder grown, on high
She curls a tendril, throws a spray, then flings
   Herself aloft in glee,
And, bursting into thousand blossoms swings
   In wreaths from tree to tree.

The dwarf-palmetto on his knees adores
   This Princess of the air;
The lone pine-barren broods afar and sighs,
   "Ah! come, lest I despair;"

The myrtle-thickets and ill-tempered thorns
    Quiver and thrill within,
As through their leaves they feel the dainty touch
    Of yellow jessamine.

The garden-roses wonder as they see
    The wreaths of golden bloom,
Brought in from the far woods with eager haste
    To deck the poorest room,
The rich man's house, alike; the loaded hands
    Give sprays to all they meet,
Till, gay with flowers, the people come and go,
    And all the air is sweet.

The Southern land, well weary of its green
    Which may not fall nor fade,
Bestirs itself to greet the lovely flower
    With leaves of fresher shade;
The pine has tassels, and the orange-trees
    Their fragrant work begin:
The spring has come—has come to Florida,
    With yellow jessamine.

INA DONNA COOLBRITH (1841–1928)

The daughter of Mormon parents, Ina Donna Coolbrith was born in Illinois and grew up in California. Coolbrith taught school for a time and then began to publish her writing in local newspapers. She was quite popular locally, and Bret Harte gave her an editing job in 1868 at the *Overland Monthly*. Coolbrith's poems began to appear nationally, in such magazines as *Harper's*, *Scribner's*, and *Putnam's*, and a book of her poems, *A Perfect Day*, was published in 1881. Coolbrith worked as a librarian at the Oakland Public Library for over twenty years. Fire destroyed her home and most of her writings in April 1906. In 1915, she summoned a World Congress of Authors and, in the same year, she was named poet laureate of California.

When the Grass Shall Cover Me

When the grass shall cover me,
Head to foot where I am lying;
    When not any wind that blows,
    Summer blooms nor winter snows,
Shall awake me to your sighing:
    Close above me as you pass,
    You will say, "How kind she was,"
    You will say, "How true she was,"
When the grass grows over me.

When the grass shall cover me,
Holden close to earth's warm bosom,—
    While I laugh, or weep, or sing
    Nevermore, for anything,
You will find in blade and blossom,
    Sweet small voices, odorous,
    Tender pleaders in my cause,
    That shall speak me as I was—
When the grass grows over me.

When the grass shall cover me!
Ah, belovèd, in my sorrow
    Very patient, I can wait,
    Knowing that, or soon or late,
There will dawn a clearer morrow:
    When your heart will moan "Alas!
    Now I know how true she was;
    Now I know how dear she was"—
When the grass grows over me!

Helen Hunt Jackson

What songs found voice upon those lips,
   What magic dwelt within the pen,
Whose music into silence slips,
   Whose spell lives not again!

For her the clamorous to-day
   The dreamful yesterday became;
The brands upon dead hearths that lay
   Leaped into living flame.

Clear ring the silvery Mission bells
   Their calls to vesper and to mass;
O'er vineyard slopes, through fruited dells,
   The long processions pass;

The pale Franciscan lifts in air
   The Cross above the kneeling throng;
Their simple world how sweet with prayer,
   With chant and matin-song!

There, with her dimpled, lifted hands,
   Parting the mustard's golden plumes,
The dusky maid, Ramona, stands
   Amid the sea of blooms.

And Alessandro, type of all
   His broken tribe, for evermore
An exile, hears the stranger call
   Within his father's door.

The visions vanish and are not,
   Still are the sounds of peace and strife,—
Passed with the earnest heart and thought
   Which lured them back to life.

O sunset land! O land of vine,
   And rose, and bay! in silence here
Let fall one little leaf of thine,
   With love, upon her bier.

Fruitionless

Ah! little flower, upspringing, azure-eyed,
  The meadow-brook beside,
    Dropping delicious balms
    Into the tender palms
Of lover-winds, that woo with light caress,
  In still contentedness,
Living and blooming thy brief summer-day: —
    So, wiser far than I,
    That only dream and sigh,
And, sighing, dream my listless life away.

Ah! sweetheart birds, a-building your wee house
  In the broad-leavëd boughs,
    Pausing with merry trill
    To praise each other's skill,
And nod your pretty heads with pretty pride;
  Serenely satisfied
To trill and twitter love's sweet roundelay: —
    So, happier than I,
    That, lonely, dream and sigh,
And, sighing, dream my lonely life away.

Brown-bodied bees, that scent with nostrils fine
  The odorous blossom-wine,
    Sipping, with heads half thrust
    Into the pollen dust
Of rose and hyacinth and daffodil,
  To hive, in amber cell,
A honey feasting for the winter-day: —
    So, better far than I,
    Self-wrapt, that dream and sigh,
And, sighing, dream my useless life away.

EMMA LAZARUS (1849–1887)

Of Portuguese Jewish ancestry, Emma Lazarus was born in New York City to wealthy parents. She began writing poems as a teenager and her first book, *Poems and Translations*, was published in 1867. Influenced by the persecution of Russian Jews, Lazarus infused much of her writings with Jewish themes. Lazarus's fame is immortalized by her timeless sonnet inscribed on the base of the Statue of Liberty. "The New Colossus," written in 1883, is a well-known and powerful statement of what it means to be an American. Other works by Lazarus include *Admetus and Other Poems* (1871), *Songs of a Semite* (1882), and a series of prose poems entitled *By the Waters of Babylon* (1887).

The New Colossus

Not like the brazen giant of Greek fame,
With conquering limbs astride from land to land;
Here at our sea-washed, sunset gates shall stand
A mighty woman with a torch, whose flame
Is the imprisoned lightning, and her name
Mother of Exiles. From her beacon-hand
Glows world-wide welcome; her mild eyes command
The air-bridged harbor that twin cities frame.
"Keep, ancient lands, your storied pomp!" cries she
With silent lips. "Give me your tired, your poor,
Your huddled masses yearning to breathe free,
The wretched refuse of your teeming shore.
Send these, the homeless, tempest-tost to me,
I lift my lamp beside the golden door!"

1492

Thou two-faced year, Mother of Change and Fate,
Didst weep when Spain cast forth with flaming sword,
The children of the prophets of the Lord,
Prince, priest, and people, spurned by zealot hate.
Hounded from sea to sea, from state to state,
The West refused them, and the East abhorred.
No anchorage the known world could afford,
Close-locked was every port, barred every gate.

Then smiling, thou unveil'dst, O two-faced year,
A virgin world where doors of sunset part,

Saying, "Ho, all who weary, enter here!
There falls each ancient barrier that the art
Of race or creed or rank devised, to rear
Grim bulwarked hatred between heart and heart!"

Echoes

Late-born and woman-souled I dare not hope,
The freshness of the elder lays, the might
Of manly, modern passion shall alight
Upon my Muse's lips, nor may I cope
(Who veiled and screened by womanhood must grope)
With the world's strong-armed warriors and recite
The dangers, wounds, and triumphs of the fight;
Twanging the full-stringed lyre through all its scope.
But if thou ever in some lake-floored cave
O'erbrowed by rocks, a wild voice wooed and heard,
Answering at once from heaven and earth and wave,
Lending elf-music to thy harshest word,
Misprize thou not these echoes that belong
To one in love with solitude and song.

The South

Night, and beneath star-blazoned summer skies
    Behold the Spirit of the musky South,
A creole with still-burning, languid eyes,
    Voluptuous limbs and incense-breathing mouth:
        Swathed in spun gauze is she,
From fibres of her own anana tree.

Within these sumptuous woods she lies at ease,
    By rich night-breezes, dewy cool, caressed:
'Twixt cypresses and slim palmetto trees,
    Like to the golden oriole's hanging nest,
        Her airy hammock swings,
And through the dark her mocking-bird yet sings.

How beautiful she is! A tulip-wreath
    Twines round her shadowy, free-floating hair:
Young, weary, passionate, and sad as death,

Dark visions haunt for her the vacant air,
     While movelessly she lies
With lithe, lax, folded hands and heavy eyes.

Full well knows she how wide and fair extend
     Her groves bright-flowered, her tangled everglades,
Majestic streams that indolently wend
     Through lush savanna or dense forest shades,
          Where the brown buzzard flies
To broad bayous 'neath hazy-golden skies.

Hers is the savage splendor of the swamp,
     With pomp of scarlet and of purple bloom,
Where blow warm, furtive breezes faint and damp,
     Strange insects whir, and stalking bitterns boom—
          Where from stale waters dead
Oft looms the great-jawed alligator's head.

Her wealth, her beauty, and the blight on these,—
     Of all she is aware: luxuriant woods,
Fresh, living, sunlit, in her dream she sees;
     And ever midst those verdant solitudes
          The soldier's wooden cross,
O'ergrown by creeping tendrils and rank moss.

Was hers a dream of empire? was it sin?
     And is it well that all was borne in vain?
She knows no more than one who slow doth win,
     After fierce fever, conscious life again,
          Too tired, too weak, too sad,
By the new light to be or stirred or glad.

From rich sea-islands fringing her green shore,
     From broad plantations where swart freemen bend
Bronzed backs in willing labor, from her store
     Of golden fruit, from stream, from town, ascend
          Life-currents of pure health:
Her aims shall be subserved with boundless wealth.

Yet now how listless and how still she lies,
     Like some half-savage, dusky Italian queen,
Rocked in her hammock 'neath her native skies,
     With the pathetic, passive, broken mien
          Of one who, sorely proved,
Great-souled, hath suffered much and much hath loved!

But look! along the wide-branched, dewy glade
   Glimmers the dawn: the light palmetto-trees
And cypresses reissue from the shade,
    And *she* hath wakened. Through clear air she sees
      The pledge, the brightening ray,
And leaps from dreams to hail the coming day.

Gifts

"O World-God, give me Wealth!" the Egyptian cried.
His prayer was granted. High as heaven, behold
Palace and Pyramid; the brimming tide
Of lavish Nile washed all his land with gold.
Armies of slaves toiled ant-wise at his feet,
World-circling traffic roared through mart and street,
His priests were gods, his spice-balmed kings enshrined,
Set death at naught in rock-ribbed charnels deep.
Seek Pharaoh's race to-day and ye shall find
Rust and the moth, silence and dusty sleep.

"O World-God, give me Beauty!" cried the Greek.
His prayer was granted. All the earth became
Plastic and vocal to his sense; each peak,
Each grove, each stream, quick with Promethean flame,
Peopled the world with imaged grace and light.
The lyre was his, and his the breathing might
Of the immortal marble, his the play
Of diamond-pointed thought and golden tongue.
Go seek the sun-shine race, ye find to-day
A broken column and a lute unstrung.

"O World-God, give me Power!" the Roman cried.
His prayer was granted. The vast world was chained
A captive to the chariot of his pride.
The blood of myriad provinces was drained
To feed that fierce, insatiable red heart.
Invulnerably bulwarked every part
With serried legions and with close-meshed code,
Within, the burrowing worm had gnawed its home,
A roofless ruin stands where once abode
The imperial race of everlasting Rome.

"O Godhead, give me Truth!" the Hebrew cried.
His prayer was granted; he became the slave
Of the Idea, a pilgrim far and wide,
Cursed, hated, spurned, and scourged with none to save.
The Pharaohs knew him, and when Greece beheld,
His wisdom wore the hoary crown of Eld.
Beauty he hath forsworn, and wealth and power.
Seek him to-day, and find in every land.
No fire consumes him, neither floods devour;
Immortal through the lamp within his hand.

The New Ezekiel

What, can these dead bones live, whose sap is dried
 By twenty scorching centuries of wrong?
Is this the House of Israel, whose pride
 Is as a tale that's told, an ancient song?
Are these ignoble relics all that live
 Of psalmist, priest, and prophet? Can the breath
Of very heaven bid these bones revive,
 Open the graves and clothe the ribs of death?

Yea, Prophesy, the Lord hath said. Again
 Say to the wind, Come forth and breathe afresh,
Even that they may live upon these slain,
 And bone to bone shall leap, and flesh to flesh.
The Spirit is not dead, proclaim the word,
 Where lay dead bones, a host of armed men stand!
I ope your graves, my people, saith the Lord,
 And I shall place you living in your land.

SARAH ORNE JEWETT (1849–1909)

Born in South Berwick, Maine, Sarah Orne Jewett was the second daughter of a highly respected physician. Accompanying her father on house calls, Jewett learned about her home state and its people. This served as a background for Jewett's later short stories. She contributed local-color stories to the *Atlantic Monthly*, and published many books over the next twenty-five years: *Deephaven* (1877), *A Country Doctor* (1884), *A White Heron and Other Stories* (1886), and *The Country of the Pointed Firs* (1896). Jewett was a prominent figure in the literary community, and was friends with other authors such as James Russell Lowell, Harriet Beecher Stowe, John Greenleaf Whittier, and Willa Cather. She died of a stroke at her family home in Maine in 1909.

A Caged Bird

High at the window in her cage
    The old canary flits and sings,
Nor sees across the curtain pass
    The shadow of a swallow's wings.

A poor deceit and copy, this,
    Of larger lives that mark their span,
Unreckoning of wider worlds
    Or gifts that Heaven keeps for man.

She gathers piteous bits and shreds,
    This solitary, mateless thing,
To patient build again the nest
    So rudely scattered spring by spring;

And sings her brief, unlistened songs,
    Her dreams of bird life wild and free,
Yet never beats her prison bars
    At sound of song from bush or tree.

But in my busiest hours I pause,
    Held by a sense of urgent speech,
Bewildered by that spark-like soul,
    Able my very soul to reach.

She will be heard; she chirps me loud,
    When I forget those gravest cares,
Her small provision to supply,
    Clear water or her seedsman's wares.

She begs me now for that chief joy
    The round great world is made to grow,—
Her wisp of greenness. Hear her chide,
    Because my answering thought is slow!

What can my life seem like to her?
    A dull, unpunctual service mine;
Stupid before her eager call,
    Her flitting steps, her insight fine.

To open wide thy prison door,
    Poor friend, would give thee to thy foes;
And yet a plaintive note I hear,
    As if to tell how slowly goes

The time of thy long prisoning.
    Bird! does some promise keep thee sane?
Will there be better days for thee?
    Will thy soul too know life again?

Ah, none of us have more than this:
    If one true friend green leaves can reach
From out some fairer, wider place,
    And understand our wistful speech!

ELLA WHEELER WILCOX (1850–1919)

Ella Wheeler Wilcox, born in Johnstown Center, Wisconsin, was educated at local public schools and attended the University of Wisconsin. At fourteen, Wilcox contributed to her family's income by publishing some sketches in the *New York Mercury*. Wilcox's first book, *Drops of Water*, was published in 1872. *Shells* (1873) and *Maurine* (1876) followed, but it was the publication of *Poems of Passion* (1883) that caused an uproar. This book of love poems was rejected by one publisher for being too racy and "immoral." Sales skyrocketed, and Wilcox continued to publish her poetry in such books as *Men, Women, and Emotions* (1893), *Poems of Pleasure* (1888), and *Poems of Power* (1901). She married in 1884, and wrote fiction stories and two autobiographies. Of her more than forty books, Wilcox is best remembered for her poem "Solitude."

Solitude

Laugh, and the world laughs with you;
   Weep, and you weep alone.
For the sad old earth must borrow its mirth,
   But has trouble enough of its own.
Sing, and the hills will answer;
   Sigh, it is lost on the air.
The echoes bound to a joyful sound,
   But shrink from voicing care.

Rejoice, and men will seek you;
   Grieve, and they turn and go.
They want full measure of all your pleasure,
   But they do not need your woe.
Be glad, and your friends are many;
   Be sad, and you lose them all.
There are none to decline your nectared wine,
   But alone you must drink life's gall.

Feast, and your halls are crowded;
   Fast, and the world goes by.
Succeed and give, and it helps you live,
   But no man can help you die.
There is room in the halls of pleasure
   For a long and lordly train,
But one by one we must all file on
   Through the narrow aisles of pain.

Individuality

O yes, I love you, and with all my heart;
Just as a weaker woman loves her own,
Better than I love my belovèd art,
Which, till you came, reigned royally, alone,
My king, my master. Since I saw your face
I have dethroned it, and you hold that place.

I am as weak as other women are—
Your frown can make the whole world like a tomb.
Your smile shines brighter than the sun, by far;
Sometimes I think there is not space or room
In all the earth for such a love as mine,
And it soars up to breathe in realms divine

I know that your desertion or neglect
Could break my heart, as women's hearts do break,
If my wan days had nothing to expect
From your love's splendor, all joy would forsake
The chambers of my soul. Yes, this is true.
And yet, and yet—one thing I keep from you.

There is a subtle part of me, which went
Into my long pursued and worshiped art;
Though your great love fills me with such content
No other love finds room now, in my heart.
Yet that rare essence was my art's alone.
Thank God you cannot grasp it; 'tis mine own.

Thank God, I say, for while I love you so,
With that vast love, as passionate as tender,
I feel an exultation as I know
I have not made you a complete surrender.
Here is my body; bruise it, if you will,
And break my heart; I have that *something* still.

You cannot grasp it. Seize the breath of morn,
Or bind the perfume of the rose as well.
God put it in my soul when I was born;
It is not mine to give away, or sell,
Or offer up on any altar shrine.
It was my art's; and when not art's, 'tis mine.

For love's sake, I can put the art away,
Or anything which stands 'twixt me and you.
But that strange essence God bestowed, I say,
To permeate the work He gave to do:
And it cannot be drained, dissolved, or sent
Through any channel, save the one He meant.

Friendship After Love

After the fierce midsummer all ablaze
   Has burned itself to ashes, and expires
   In the intensity of its own fires,
There come the mellow, mild, St. Martin days
Crowned with the calm of peace, but sad with haze.
   So after Love has led us, till he tires
   Of his own throes, and torments, and desires,
Comes large-eyed friendship: with a restful gaze,
He beckons us to follow, and across
   Cool verdant vales we wander free from care.
   Is it a touch of frost lies in the air?
Why are we haunted with a sense of loss?
We do not wish the pain back, or the heat;
And yet, and yet, these days are incomplete.

Delilah

In the midnight of darkness and terror,
When I would grope nearer to God,
With my back to a record of error
And the highway of sin I have trod,
There come to me shapes I would banish—
The shapes of the deeds I have done;
And I pray and I plead till they vanish—
All vanish and leave me, save one.

That one, with a smile like the splendor
Of the sun in the middle-day skies—
That one, with a spell that is tender—
That one with a dream in her eyes—
Cometh close, in her rare Southern beauty,
Her languor, her indolent grace;

And my soul turns its back on its duty,
To live in the light of her face.

She touches my cheek, and I quiver—
I tremble with exquisite pains;
She sighs—like an overcharged river
My blood rushes on through my veins;
She smiles—and in mad-tiger fashion,
As a she-tiger fondles her own,
I clasp her with fierceness and passion,
And kiss her with shudder and groan.

Once more, in our love's sweet beginning,
I put away God and the World;
Once more, in the joys of our sinnings,
Are the hopes of eternity hurled.
There is nothing my soul lacks or misses
As I clasp the dream-shape to my breast;
In the passion and pain of her kisses
Life blooms to its richest and best.

O ghost of dead sin unrelenting,
Go back to the dust, and the sod!
Too dear and too sweet for repenting,
Ye stand between me and my God.
If I, by the Throne, should behold you,
Smiling up with those eyes loved so well,
Close, close in my arms I would fold you,
And drop with you down to sweet Hell!

ROSE HARTWICK THORPE (1850–1939)

Rose Hartwick Thorpe was born in Indiana and grew up in Kansas and Michigan, where she attended public school. Her most famous ballad, "Curfew Must Not Ring To-Night," was written when Thorpe was a teenager, and was first published in the *Commercial Advertiser* in Detroit in 1870. Based on a short story from *Peterson's Magazine,* the narrative poem was immensely popular, and an illustrated edition appeared in 1882. Thorpe married in 1871, and continued submitting poetry to periodicals while raising her two daughters. After her husband's death, she worked for women's suffrage and was a member of the Women's Club of San Diego. In addition to her verse, published in *Temperance Poems* (1887), *Ringing Ballads* (1887), and *The Poetical Works of Rose Hartwick Thorpe* (1912), Thorpe also wrote a number of books for children.

Curfew Must Not Ring To-Night

England's sun was slowly setting o'er the hill-tops far away,
Filling all the land with beauty at the close of one sad day;
And its last rays kissed the forehead of a man and maiden fair,—
He with steps so slow and weary, she with sunny, floating hair:
He with bowed head, sad and thoughtful; she with lips so cold and
    white,
Struggled to keep back the murmur, "Curfew must not ring to-night!"

"Sexton," Bessie's white lips faltered, pointing to the prison old,
With its walls so tall and gloomy,—moss-grown walls dark, damp, and
    cold,—
"I've a lover in that prison, doomed this very night to die
At the ringing of the curfew, and no earthly help is nigh.
Cromwell will not come till sunset"; and her lips grew strangely white
As she spoke in husky whispers, "Curfew must not ring to-night!"

"Bessie," calmly spoke the sexton (every word pierced her young heart
Like a gleaming death-winged arrow, like a deadly poisoned dart),
"Long, long years I've rung the curfew from that gloomy, shadowed
    tower;
Every evening, just at sunset, it has tolled the twilight hour.
I have done my duty ever, tried to do it just and right;
Now I'm old I will not miss it: Curfew bell must ring to-night!"

Wild her eyes and pale her features, stern and white her thoughtful
    brow,
And within her heart's deep centre Bessie made a solemn vow.
She had listened while the judges read, without a tear or sigh,

"At the ringing of the curfew Basil Underwood *must die*."
And her breath came fast and faster, and her eyes grew large and
     bright;
One low murmur, faintly spoken, "Curfew *must not* ring to-night!"

She with quick step bounded forward, sprang within the old church
     door,
Left the old man coming, slowly, paths he'd trod so oft before.
Not one moment paused the maiden, but, with cheek and brow
     aglow,
Staggered up the gloomy tower where the bell swung to and fro;
As she climbed the slimy ladder, on which fell no ray of light,
Upward still, her pale lips saying, "Curfew *shall not* ring to-night!"

She has reached the topmost ladder; o'er her hangs the great, dark
     bell;
Awful is the gloom beneath her, like the pathway down to hell.
See, the ponderous tongue is swinging! 't is the hour of curfew now!
And the sight has chilled her bosom, stopped her breath and paled
     her brow.
Shall she let it ring? No, never! Her eyes flash with sudden light,
As she springs and grasps it firmly: "Curfew *shall not* ring to-night!"

Out she swung, far out; the city seemed a speck of light below,
There 'twixt heaven and earth suspended, as the bell swung to and
     fro.
And the sexton at the bell-rope, old and deaf, heard not the bell;
Sadly thought that twilight curfew rang young Basil's funeral knell.
Still the maiden, clinging firmly, quivering lip and fair face white,
Stilled her frightened heart's wild beating: "*Curfew shall not ring to-
     night!*"

It was o'er!—the bell ceased swaying, and the maiden stepped once
     more
Firmly on the damp old ladder, where, for hundred years before,
Human foot had not been planted. The brave deed that she had done
Should be told long ages after. As the rays of setting sun
Light the sky with golden beauty, aged sires, with heads of white,
Tell the children why the curfew did not ring that one sad night.

O'er the distant hills comes Cromwell. Bessie sees him, and her
     brow,
Lately white with sickening horror, has no anxious traces now.

At his feet she tells her story, shows her hands, all bruised and torn;
And her sweet young face, still haggard with the anguish it had worn,
Touched his heart with sudden pity, lit his eyes with misty light.
"Go! your lover lives," cried Cromwell. "Curfew shall not ring to-
    night!"

Wide they flung the massive portals, led the prisoner forth to die,
All his bright young life before him, 'neath the darkening English sky.
Bessie came, with flying footsteps, eyes aglow with lovelight sweet,
Kneeling on the turf beside him, laid his pardon at his feet.
In his brave, strong arms he clasped her, kissed the face upturned and
    white,
Whispered, "Darling, you have saved me! curfew will not ring to-
    night."

ROSE HAWTHORNE LATHROP (1851–1926)

The youngest child of author Nathaniel Hawthorne, Rose Hawthorne Lathrop was born in Lenox, Massachusetts, and lived in England, Portugal, and Italy before marrying in 1871. Between 1875 and 1892, Lathrop published fiction for children as well as poetry on the themes of relationships, death, and grief. After converting to Roman Catholicism, she began writing about issues of social justice. In 1896, Lathrop founded an order of nuns to help care for indigents dying of cancer. From then on, Lathrop was known as Mother Mary Alphonsa.

A Song Before Grief

Sorrow, my friend,
When shall you come again?
The wind is slow, and the bent willows send
Their silvery motions wearily down the plain.
The bird is dead
That sang this morning through the summer rain!

Sorrow, my friend,
I owe my soul to you.
And if my life with any glory end
Of tenderness for others, and the words are true,
Said, honoring, when I'm dead,—
Sorrow, to you, the mellow praise, the funeral wreath, are due.

And yet, my friend,
When love and joy are strong,
Your terrible visage from my sight I rend
With glances to blue heaven. Hovering along,
By mine your shadow led,
"Away!" I shriek, "nor dare to work my new-sprung mercies wrong!"

Still, you are near:
Who can your care withstand?
When deep eternity shall look most clear,
Sending bright waves to kiss the trembling land,
My joy shall disappear,—
A flaming torch thrown to the golden sea by your pale hand.

KATE NICHOLS TRASK (1853–1922)

Kate Nichols Trask, born in Brooklyn, New York, to a wealthy family, was educated in private schools and married a banker in 1874. After her children died, Trask turned to writing, and published three long love poems anonymously in 1892. All of her subsequent books, including *Sonnets and Lyrics* (1894), *White Satin and Homespun* (1896), *Free, Not Bound* (1903), and *In the Vanguard* (1914), an anti-war play, were signed with the name "Katrina Trask." She was also very active in various philanthropies. As early as 1899, Trask and her husband hoped to open their large Saratoga Springs estate, Yaddo, as an artists' colony. After Trask's death in 1922, Yaddo served as a summer retreat for artists.

Sorrow

O thorn-crowned Sorrow, pitiless and stern,
I sit alone with broken heart, my head
Low bowed, keeping long vigil with my dead.
My soul, unutterably sad, doth yearn
Beyond relief in tears—they only burn
My aching eyelids to fall back unshed
Upon the throbbing brain like molten lead,
Making it frenzied. Shall I ever learn
To face you fearlessly, as by my door
You stand with haunting eyes and death-damp hair,
Through the night-watches, whispering solemnly,
"Behold, I am thy guest forevermore."
It chills my soul to know that you are there.
Great God, have mercy on my misery!

Aidenn

Heaven is mirrored, Love, deep in thine eyes,
Soft falls its shimmering light upon thy face;
Tell me, Beloved, is this Paradise,
Or but Love's bower in some deep-sheltered place?

Is that God's burning bush that now appears,
Or but the sunlight slanting through the trees?
Is that sweet song the music of the spheres,
Or but the deep andante of the breeze?

Are we blest spirits of some glad new birth
Floating at last in God's eternity?
Or art thou, Love, still but a man on earth,
And I a woman clinging close to thee?

EDITH M. THOMAS (1854–1925)

Edith M. Thomas, born in Chatham, Ohio, wrote poems at an early age, greatly inspired by the poetry of John Keats and her appreciation of Greek literature. She taught school for two years and worked as a typesetter before visiting New York City in 1881. While there, Thomas met Helen Hunt Jackson, who encouraged her to contribute her poems to *Century* magazine and the *Atlantic Monthly*. Her first collection, *A New Year's Masque*, was published in 1885, and was followed by many more successful books, such as *Lyrics and Sonnets* (1887), *The Inverted Torch* (1890), and several books for children.

The Mother Who Died Too

She was so little—little in her grave,
  The wide earth all around so hard and cold—
She was so little! therefore did I crave
  My arms might still her tender form enfold.
She was so little, and her cry so weak
  When she among the heavenly children came—
She was so little—I alone might speak
  For her who knew no word nor her own name.

Winter Sleep

I know it must be winter (though I sleep)—
  I know it must be winter, for I dream
  I dip my bare feet in the running stream,
And flowers are many, and the grass grows deep.

I know I must be old (how age deceives!)—
  I know I must be old, for, all unseen,
  My heart grows young, as autumn fields grow green,
When late rains patter on the falling sheaves.

I know I must be tired (and tired souls err)—
  I know I must be tired, for all my soul
  To deeds of daring beats a glad, faint roll,
As storms the riven pine to music stir.

I know I must be dying (Death draws near)—
  I know I must be dying, for I crave
  Life—life, strong life, and think not of the grave,
And turf-bound silence, in the frosty year.

LIZETTE WOODWORTH REESE (1856–1935)

Maryland-born Lizette Woodworth Reese attended St. John's Parish School and the public schools of Baltimore. She was a teacher for forty-five years, and her leisure time was devoted to writing poetry. "The Deserted House" was her first published poem, appearing in the *Southern Magazine* in 1874. Her first book of poems, *A Branch of May*, was published thirteen years later, in 1887. Among Reese's fourteen books are: *A Handful of Lavender* (1891), *A Quiet Road* (1896), and *Spicewood* (1920). "Tears" is her most famous sonnet, first appearing in *Scribner's Magazine* in 1899. Reese also published two books of her memoirs entitled *A Victorian Village* (1929) and *The York Road* (1931). In 1931, Reese received the Mary L. Keats Memorial Prize and was named poet laureate of Maryland.

One Night

One lily scented all the dark. It grew
Down the drenched walk a spike of ghostly white.
Fine, sweet, sad noises thrilled the tender night,
From insects couched on blades that dripped with dew.
The road beyond, cleaving the great fields through,
Echoed no footstep; like a streak of light,
The gaunt and blossoming elder gleamed in sight.
The boughs began to quake, and warm winds blew,
And whirled a myriad petals down the air.
An instant, peaked and black the old house stood;
The next, its gables showed a tremulous gray,
Then deepening gold; the next, the world lay bare!
The moon slipped out the leash of the tall wood,
And through the heavenly meadows fled away.

Tears

When I consider Life and its few years—
A wisp of fog betwixt us and the sun;
A call to battle, and the battle done
Ere the last echo dies within our ears;
A rose choked in the grass; an hour of fears;
The gusts that past a darkening shore do beat;
The burst of music down an unlistening street—
I wonder at the idleness of tears.
Ye old, old dead, and ye of yesternight,
Chieftains, and bards, and keepers of the sheep,
By every cup of sorrow that you had,

Loose me from tears, and make me see aright
How each hath back what once he stayed to weep;
Homer his sight, David his little lad!

Spicewood

The spicewood burns along the gray, spent sky,
In moist unchimneyed places, in a wind,
That whips it all before, and all behind,
Into one thick, rude flame, now low, now high.
It is the first, the homeliest thing of all—
At sight of it, that lad that by it fares,
Whistles afresh his foolish, town-caught airs—
A thing so honey-colored and so tall!

It is as though the young Year, ere he pass,
To the white riot of the cherry tree,
Would fain accustom us, or here, or there,
To his new sudden ways with bough and grass,
So starts with what is humble, plain to see,
And all familiar as a cup, a chair.

KATHARINE LEE BATES (1859–1929)

Famous for writing the unofficial national hymn, Katharine Lee Bates wrote "America the Beautiful" after climbing Pike's Peak while on a western tour in 1893. It was first published in the *Congregationalist* in July 1895 and revised in the *Boston Evening Transcript* in November 1904. It appeared in its final form in 1911. The poem was set to the music of Samuel A. Ward's "Materna." Born in Falmouth, Massachusetts, Bates was graduated from Wellesley College in 1880 and worked as a professor of English there for forty years. She retired as professor emeritus in 1925. In addition to her work as an educator, Bates also wrote children's stories, travel books, and scholarly works.

America the Beautiful

O beautiful for spacious skies,
    For amber waves of grain,
For purple mountain majesties
    Above the fruited plain!
      America! America!
    God shed His grace on thee
And crown thy good with brotherhood
    From sea to shining sea!

O beautiful for pilgrim feet,
    Whose stern, impassioned stress
A thoroughfare for freedom beat
    Across the wilderness!
      America! America!
    God mend thine every flaw,
Confirm thy soul in self-control,
    Thy liberty in law!

O beautiful for heroes proved
    In liberating strife,
Who more than self their country loved,
    And mercy more than life!
      America! America!
    May God thy gold refine,
Till all success be nobleness,
    And every gain divine!

O beautiful for patriot dream
    That sees beyond the years
Thine alabaster cities gleam

Undimmed by human tears!
America! America!
God shed His grace on thee
And crown thy good with brotherhood
From sea to shining sea!

CHARLOTTE PERKINS GILMAN (1860–1935)

Charlotte Perkins Gilman, a leading American feminist and economist, was born in Hartford, Connecticut. At eighteen, Gilman attended the Rhode Island School of Design and worked as a teacher and commercial artist. After divorcing her first husband, artist Charles Walter Stetson, in 1894, she lectured on women's issues in California. She wrote *The Yellow Wallpaper* in 1892 and her only book of poems, *In This Our World*, the following year. She earned critical acclaim for her 1898 book *Women and Economics*, which attacked women's financial dependency on men. Gilman remarried in 1902 and continued to publish her stories in various periodicals, including her journal, *The Forerunner*. In 1932, Gilman was diagnosed with breast cancer; she took her own life on August 17, 1935.

A Common Inference

A night: mysterious, tender, quiet, deep;
Heavy with flowers; full of life asleep;
Thrilling with insect voices; thick with stars;
No cloud between the dewdrops and red Mars;
The small earth whirling softly on her way,
The moonbeams and the waterfalls at play;
A million million worlds that move in peace,
A million mighty laws that never cease;
And one small ant-heap, hidden by small weeds,
Rich with eggs, slaves, and store of millet seeds.
     They sleep beneath the sod
       And trust in God.

A day: all glorious, royal, blazing bright;
Heavy with flowers; full of life and light;
Great fields of corn and sunshine; courteous trees;
Snow-sainted mountains; earth-embracing seas;
Wide golden deserts; slender silver streams;
Clear rainbows where the tossing fountain gleams;
And everywhere, in happiness and peace,
A million forms of life that never cease;
And one small ant-heap, crushed by passing tread,
Hath scarce enough alive to mourn the dead!
     They shriek beneath the sod,
       "There is no God!"

The Beds of Fleur-de-lys

High-lying, sea-blown stretches of green turf,
　Wind-bitten close, salt-colored by the sea,
Low curve on curve spread far to the cool sky,
And, curving over them as long they lie,
　Beds of wild fleur-de-lys.

Wide-flowing, self-sown, stealing near and far,
　Breaking the green like islands in the sea;
Great stretches at your feet, and spots that bend
Dwindling over the horizon's end,—
　Wild beds of fleur-de-lys.

The light keen wind streams on across the lifts,
　Their wind of western springtime by the sea;
The close turf smiles unmoved, but over her
Is the far-flying rustle and sweet stir
　In beds of fleur-de-lys.

And here and there across the smooth, low grass
　Tall maidens wander, thinking of the sea;
And bend, and bend, with light robes blown aside,
For the blue lily-flowers that bloom so wide,—
　The beds of fleur-de-lys.

A Conservative

The garden beds I wandered by
　One bright and cheerful morn,
When I found a new-fledged butterfly,
　A-sitting on a thorn,
A black and crimson butterfly,
　All doleful and forlorn.

I thought that life could have no sting
　To infant butterflies,
So I gazed on this unhappy thing
　With wonder and surprise,
While sadly with his waving wing
　He wiped his weeping eyes.

Said I, "What can the matter be?
　Why weepest thou so sore?

With garden fair and sunlight free
  And flowers in goodly store:"—
But he only turned away from me
  And burst into a roar.

Cried he, "My legs are thin and few
  Where once I had a swarm!
Soft fuzzy fur—a joy to view—
  Once kept my body warm,
Before these flapping wing-things grew,
  To hamper and deform!"

At that outrageous bug I shot
  The fury of mine eye;
Said I, in scorn all burning hot,
  In rage and anger high,
"You ignominious idiot!
  Those wings are made to fly!"

"I do not want to fly," said he,
  "I only want to squirm!"
And he drooped his wings dejectedly,
  But still his voice was firm:
"I do not want to be a fly!
  I want to be a worm!"

O yesterday of unknown lack!
  To-day of unknown bliss!
I left my fool in red and black,
  The last I saw was this,—
The creature madly climbing back
  Into his chrysalis.

HARRIET MONROE (1860–1936)

With literary mentors like Robert Louis Stevenson, William Dean Howells, and Edmund Clarence Stedman, Harriet Monroe submitted her poetry to *Century* magazine, and wrote a cantata for the dedication of a theater in Chicago. In 1891, Monroe published *Valeria and Other Poems*. Later that year, she was asked to write the "Columbian Ode" for the opening of the World's Columbian Exposition in Chicago in 1892. The poems, recited to commemorate the 400th anniversary of the discovery of America, were published in 1893. Monroe's greatest contribution was her *Poetry: A Magazine of Verse*, which first appeared in October, 1912, and showcased both well-known poets and fresh, young voices. Collaborating with Alice Corbin Henderson, Monroe published some free verse in her anthology, *The New Poetry* (1917; revised 1932). Her autobiography, *A Poet's Life*, appeared in 1938.

To W. S. M.

With a copy of Shelley.

Behold, I send thee to the heights of song,
My brother! Let thine eyes awake as clear
As morning dew, within whose glowing sphere
Is mirrored half a world; and listen long,
Till in thine ears, famished to keenness, throng
The bugles of the soul—till far and near
Silence grows populous, and wind and mere
Are phantom-choked with voices. Then be strong—
Then halt not till thou seest the beacons flare
Souls mad for truth have lit from peak to peak.
Haste on to breathe the intoxicating air—
Wine to the brave and poison to the weak—
Far in the blue where angels' feet have trod,
Where earth is one with heaven, and man with God.

A Farewell

Good-by: nay, do not grieve that it is over—
    The perfect hour;
That the winged joy, sweet honey-loving rover,
    Flits from the flower.

Grieve not,—it is the law. Love will be flying—
    Yea, love and all.
Glad was the living; blessed be the dying!
    Let the leaves fall.

Love Song

I love my life, but not too well
  To give it to thee like a flower,
So it may pleasure thee to dwell
  Deep in its perfume but an hour.
I love my life, but not too well.

I love my life, but not too well
  To sing it note by note away,
So to thy soul the song may tell
  The beauty of the desolate day.
I love my life, but not too well.

I love my life, but not too well
  To cast it like a cloak on thine,
Against the storms that sound and swell
  Between thy lonely heart and mine.
I love my life, but not too well.

Washington

When dreaming kings, at odds with swift-paced time,
  Would strike that banner down,
A nobler knight than ever writ or rhyme
  With fame's bright wreath did crown
Through armed hosts bore it till it floated high
Beyond the clouds, a light that cannot die!
  Ah, hero of our younger race!
    Great builder of a temple new!
  Ruler, who sought no lordly place!
    Warrior, who sheathed the sword he drew!
Lover of men, who saw afar
A world unmarred by want or war,
Who knew the path, and yet forbore
To tread, till all men should implore;
Who saw the light, and led the way
Where the gray world might greet the day;
Father and leader, prophet sure,
Whose will in vast works shall endure,
How shall we praise him on this day of days,
Great son of fame who has no need of praise?

How shall we praise him? Open wide the doors
 Of the fair temple whose broad base he laid.
 Through its white halls a shadowy cavalcade
Of heroes moves o'er unresounding floors—
Men whose brawned arms upraised these columns high,
And reared the towers that vanish in the sky,—
The strong who, having wrought, can never die.

Lincoln

And, lo! leading a blessed host comes one
 Who held a warring nation in his heart;
 Who knew love's agony, but had no part
In love's delight; whose mighty task was done
Through blood and tears that we might walk in joy,
And this day's rapture own no sad alloy.
Around him heirs of bliss, whose bright brows wear
Palm-leaves amid their laurels ever fair.
 Gaily they come, as though the drum
Beat out the call their glad hearts knew so well:
 Brothers once more, dear as of yore,
Who in a noble conflict nobly fell.
Their blood washed pure yon banner in the sky,
And quenched the brands laid 'neath these arches high—
The brave who, having fought, can never die.

Then surging through the vastness rise once more
The aureoled heirs of light, who onward bore
Through darksome times and trackless realms of ruth
The flag of beauty and the torch of truth.
They tore the mask from the foul face of wrong;
 Even to God's mysteries they dared aspire;
 High in the choir they built yon altar-fire,
And filled these aisles with color and with song:
The ever-young, the unfallen, wreathing for time
 Fresh garlands of the seeming-vanished years;
Faces long luminous, remote, sublime,
 And shining brows still dewy with our tears.
Back with the old glad smile comes one we knew—
 We bade him rear our house of joy to-day.
 But Beauty opened wide her starry way,
And he passed on. Bright champions of the true,

Soldiers of peace, seers, singers ever blest,—
From the wide ether of a loftier quest
Their winged souls throng our rites to glorify,—
The wise who, having known, can never die.

Democracy

For, lo! the living God doth bare his arm.
   No more he makes his house of clouds and gloom.
   Lightly the shuttles move within his loom;
Unveiled his thunder leaps to meet the storm.
From God's right hand man takes the powers that sway
     A universe of stars.
He bows them down; he bids them go or stay;
   He tames them for his wars
He scans the burning paces of the sun,
And names the invisible orbs whose courses run
     Through the dim deeps of space.
He sees in dew upon a rose impearled
The swarming legions of a monad world
     Begin life's upward race.
       Voices of hope he hears
     Long dumb to his despair,
      And dreams of golden years
     Meet for a world so fair.
For now Democracy doth wake and rise
     From the sweet sloth of youth.
By storms made strong, by many dreams made wise,
     He clasps the hand of Truth.
Through the armed nations lies his path of peace,
   The open book of knowledge in his hand.
Food to the starving, to the oppressed release,
   And love to all he bears from land to land.
     Before his march the barriers fall,
     The laws grow gentle at his call.
     His glowing breath blows far away
     The fogs that veil the coming day,—
       That wondrous day
When earth shall sing as through the blue she rolls
Laden with joy for all her thronging souls.
Then shall want's call to sin resound no more

Across her teeming fields. And pain shall sleep,
Soothed by brave science with her magic lore;
  And war no more shall bid the nations weep.
Then the worn chains shall slip from man's desire,
    And ever higher and higher
    His swift foot shall aspire;
    Still deeper and more deep
    His soul its watch shall keep,
Till love shall make the world a holy place,
Where knowledge dare unveil God's very face.

Not yet the angels hear life's last sweet song.
Music unutterably pure and strong
From earth shall rise to haunt the peopled skies,
    When the long march of time,
Patient in birth and death, in growth and blight,
Shall lead man up through happy realms of light
    Unto his goal sublime.

LOUISE IMOGEN GUINEY (1861–1920)

Poet and essayist Louise Imogen Guiney was born in Boston, Massachusetts. After her father's death, Guiney helped support her family by selling poems and essays to magazines. Her collections of poems include *Songs at the Start* (1884), *The White Sail and Other Poems* (1887), and *A Roadside Harp* (1893). Her essays were published in *Goose Quill Papers* (1885). Her musical verses, modeled after old English ballads and poems, were very popular in her day. Guiney also worked as a postmaster and librarian before moving to England in 1901.

The Wild Ride

I hear in my heart, I hear in its ominous pulses,
All day, on the road, the hoofs of invisible horses;
All night, from their stalls, the importunate tramping and neighing.

Let cowards and laggards fall back! but alert to the saddle,
Straight, grim, and abreast, go the weather-worn, galloping legion,
With a stirrup-cup each to the lily of women that loves him.

The trail is through dolor and dread, over crags and morasses;
There are shapes by the way, there are things that appal or entice us:
What odds? We are knights, and our souls are but bent on the riding.

I hear in my heart, I hear in its ominous pulses,
All day, on the road, the hoofs of invisible horses;
All night, from their stalls, the importunate tramping and neighing.

We spur to a land of no name, out-racing the storm-wind;
We leap to the infinite dark, like the sparks from the anvil.
Thou leadest, O God! All's well with Thy troopers that follow.

At a Symphony

Oh, I would have these tongues oracular
Dip into silence, tease no more, let be!
They madden, like some choral of the free
Gusty and sweet against a prison-bar.
To earth the boast that her gold empires are,
The menace of delicious death to me,
Great Undesign, strong as by God's decree,
Piercing the heart with beauty from afar!
Music too winning to the sense forlorn!
Of what angelic lineage was she born,

159

Bred in what rapture?—These her sires and friends:
Censure, Denial, Gloom, and Hunger's throe.
Praised be the Spirit that thro' thee, Schubert! so
Wrests evil unto wholly heavenly ends.

GRACE ELLERY CHANNING-STETSON (1862–1937)

Grace Ellery Channing-Stetson, born in Providence, Rhode Island, was educated in private schools and lived in Southern California, Italy, and New York during her lifetime. She was married in 1894 to the artist Charles Walter Stetson, who was the first husband of her best friend, Charlotte Perkins Gilman. Some of her published works include *The Sister of a Saint* (1895) and a book of verse, *Sea Drift* (1899). Channing-Stetson also edited *Dr. Channing's Note Book* (1887).

Any Woman to a Soldier

The day you march away—let the sun shine,
Let everything be blue and gold and fair,
Triumph of trumpets calling through bright air,
Flags slanting, flowers flaunting—not a sign
That the unbearable is now to bear,
          The day you march away.

The day you march away—this I have sworn,
No matter what comes after, that shall be
Hid secretly between my soul and me
As women hide the unborn—
You shall see brows like banners, lips that frame
Smiles, for the pride those lips have in your name.
You shall see soldiers in my eyes that day—
          That day, O soldier, when you march away.

The day you march away—cannot I guess?
There will be ranks and ranks, all leading on
To one white face, and then—the white face gone,
And nothing left but a gray emptiness—
Blurred moving masses, faceless, featureless—
          The day you march away.

You cannot march away! However far,
Farther and faster still I shall have fled
Before you; and that moment when you land,
Voiceless, invisible, close at your hand
My heart shall smile, hearing the steady tread
          Of your faith-keeping feet.

First at the trenches I shall be to greet;
There's not a watch I shall not share with you;
But more—but most—there where for you the red,

161

Drenched, dreadful, splendid, sacrificial field lifts up
Inflexible demand,
        I will be there!

My hands shall hold the cup.
My hands beneath your head
Shall bear you—not the stretcher bearer's—through
All anguish of the dying and the dead;
With all your wounds I shall have ached and bled,
Waked, thirsted, starved, been fevered, gasped for breath,
Felt the death dew;
And you shall live, because my heart has said
To Death
        That Death itself shall have no part in you!

EDITH WHARTON (1862–1937)

Famous as a novelist and short story writer, Edith Wharton was born into a prosperous family in New York City and was educated by governesses. At sixteen, Wharton's poems were privately printed and after her marriage in 1885, she began contributing stories and poems to *Harper's, Scribner's,* and other magazines. Of her more than fifty books, her most famous work is the novel *Ethan Frome* (1911). In 1920, Wharton won a Pulitzer Prize for another novel, *The Age of Innocence.* Some of her other books include *The Fruit of the Tree* (1907), *The Hermit and the Wild Woman* (1908), a book of short stories, *Twilight Sleep* (1927), and *A Backward Glance* (1934), an autobiography. Wharton lived in France after 1907, divorced her husband in 1913 and, in 1923, became the first woman to receive an honorary doctorate from Yale University.

The Last Giustiniani

O wife, wife, wife! As if the sacred name
Could weary one with saying! Once again
Laying against my brow your lips' soft flame,
Join with me, Sweetest, in love's new refrain,
Since the whole music of my late-found life
Is that we call each other "husband—wife."

And yet, stand back, and let your cloth of gold
Straighten its sumptuous lines from waist to knee,
And, flowing firmly outward, fold on fold,
Invest your slim young form with majesty
As when, in those calm bridal robes arrayed,
You stood beside me, and I was afraid.

I was afraid—O sweetness, whiteness, youth,
Best gift of God, I feared you! I, indeed,
For whom all womanhood has been, forsooth,
Summed up in the sole Virgin of the Creed,
I thought that day our Lady's self stood there
And bound herself to me with vow and prayer.

Ah, yes, that day. I sat, remember well,
Half-crook'd above a missal, and laid in
The gold-leaf slowly; silence in my cell;
The picture, Satan tempting Christ to sin
Upon the mount's blue, pointed pinnacle,
The world outspread beneath as fair as hell—

When suddenly they summoned me. I stood
Abashed before the Abbot, who reclined
Full-bellied in his chair beneath the rood,
And roseate with having lately dined;
And then—I standing there abashed—he said:
"The house of Giustiniani all lie dead."

It scarcely seemed to touch me (I had led
A grated life so long) that oversea
My kinsmen in their knighthood should lie dead,
Nor that this sudden death should set me free,
Me, the last Giustiniani—well, what then?
A monk!—The Giustiniani had been men.

So when the Abbot said: "The State decrees
That you, the latest scion of the house
Which died in vain for Venice overseas,
Should be exempted from your sacred vows,
And straightway, when you leave this cloistered place,
Take wife, and add new honors to the race,"

I hardly heard him—would have crept again
To the warped missal—but he snatched a sword
And girded me, and all the heart of men
Rushed through me, as he laughed and hailed me lord,
And, with my hand upon the hilt, I cried,
"Viva San Marco!" like my kin who died.

But, straightway, when, a new-made knight, I stood
Beneath the bridal arch, and saw you come,
A certain monkish warping of the blood
Ran up and struck the man's heart in me dumb;
I breathed an Ave to our Lady's grace,
And did not dare to look upon your face.

And when we swept the waters side by side,
With timbrelled gladness clashing on the air,
I trembled at your image in the tide,
And warded off the devil with a prayer,
Still seeming in a golden dream to move
Through fiendish labyrinths of forbidden love.

But when they left us, and we stood alone,
I, the last Giustiniani, face to face

With your unvisioned beauty, made my own
In this, the last strange bridal of our race,
And, looking up at last to meet your eyes,
Saw in their depths the star of love arise.

Ah, then the monk's garb shrivelled from my heart,
And left me man to face your womanhood.
Without a prayer to keep our lips apart
I turned about and kissed you where you stood,
And gathering all the gladness of my life
Into a new-found word, I called you "wife!"

Life

Life, like a marble block, is given to all,
A blank, inchoate mass of years and days,
Whence one with ardent chisel swift essays
Some shape of strength or symmetry to call;
One shatters it in bits to mend a wall;
One in a craftier hand the chisel lays,
And one, to wake the mirth in Lesbia's gaze,
Carves it apace in toys fantastical.

But least is he who, with enchanted eyes
Filled with high visions of fair shapes to be,
Muses which god he shall immortalize
In the proud Parian's perpetuity,
Till twilight warns him from the punctual skies
That the night cometh wherein none shall see.

With the Tide*

Somewhere I read, in an old book whose name
Is gone from me, I read that when the days
Of a man are counted, and his business done,
There comes up the shore at evening, with the tide,
To the place where he sits, a boat—
And in the boat, from the place where he sits, he sees,
Dim in the dusk, dim and yet so familiar,
The faces of his friends long dead; and knows

---

*This poem was written the day after Theodore Roosevelt died.

They come for him, brought in upon the tide,
To take him where men go at set of day.
Then rising, with his hands in theirs, he goes
Between them his last steps, that are the first
Of the new life—and with the ebb they pass,
Their shaken sail grown small upon the moon.

Often I thought of this, and pictured me
How many a man who lives with throngs about him,
Yet straining through the twilight for that boat
Shall scarce make out one figure in the stern,
And that so faint its features shall perplex him
With doubtful memories—and his heart hang back.
But others, rising as they see the sail
Increase upon the sunset, hasten down,
Hands out and eyes elated; for they see
Head over head, crowding from bow to stern,
Repeopling their long loneliness with smiles,
The faces of their friends; and such go forth
Content upon the ebb tide, with safe hearts.

But never
To worker summoned when his day was done
Did mounting tide bring in such freight of friends
As stole to you up the white wintry shingle
    That night while they that watched you thought you slept.
Softly they came, and beached the boat, and gathered
In the still cove under the icy stars,
Your last-born, and the dear loves of your heart,
And all men that have loved right more than ease,
And honor above honors; all who gave
Free-handed of their best for other men,
And thought their giving taking: they who knew
Man's natural state is effort, up and up—
All these were there, so great a company
Perchance you marvelled, wondering what great ship
Had brought that throng unnumbered to the cove
Where the boys used to beach their light canoe
After old happy picnics—

But these, your friends and children, to whose hands
Committed, in the silent night you rose

And took your last faint steps—
These led you down, O great American,
Down to the Winter night and the white beach,
And there you saw that the huge hull that waited
Was not as are the boats of the other dead,
Frail craft for a brief passage; no, for this
Was first of a long line of towering transports,
Storm-worn and ocean-weary every one,
The ships you launched, the ships you manned, the ships
That now, returning from their sacred quest
With the thrice-sacred burden of their dead,
Lay waiting there to take you forth with them,
Out with the ebb tide, on some farther quest.

WILLA CATHER (1873–1947)

Known primarily for her fiction novels such as *Alexander's Bridge* (1912), *O Pioneers!* (1913), and *My Antonia* (1918), Willa Cather was born in Virginia and moved to frontier Nebraska when she was a child. Cather managed and edited the *Home Monthly* magazine in 1896–97 and reviewed drama and music for the *Pittsburgh Daily Leader*. Cather became a schoolteacher in 1901 and published her poetry book, *April Twilights*, in 1903. Her 1905 collection of short stories, *The Troll Garden*, earned her the job of managing editor of *McClure's Magazine*.

"Grandmither, think not I forget!"

Grandmither, think not I forget, when I come back to town,
An' wander the old ways again an' tread them up an' down.
I never smell the clover bloom, nor see the swallows pass,
Without I mind how good ye were unto a little lass.
I never hear the winter rain a-pelting all night through,
Without I think and mind me of how cold it falls on you.
And if I come not often to your bed beneath the thyme,
Mayhap 't is that I'd change wi' ye, and gie my bed for thine,
      Would like to sleep in thine.

I never hear the summer winds among the roses blow,
Without I wonder why it was ye loved the lassie so.
Ye gave me cakes and lollipops and pretty toys a score,—
I never thought I should come back and ask ye now for more.
Grandmither, gie me your still, white hands, that lie upon your breast,
For mine do beat the dark all night and never find me rest;
They grope among the shadows an' they beat the cold black air,
They go seekin' in the darkness, an' they never find him there,
      As They never find him there.

Grandmither, gie me your sightless eyes, that I may never see
His own a-burnin' full o' love that must not shine for me.
Grandmither, gie me your peaceful lips, white as the kirkyard snow,
For mine be red wi' burnin' thirst an' he must never know.
Grandmither, gie me your clay-stopped ears, that I may never hear
My lad a-singin' in the night when I am sick wi' fear;
A-singing when the moonlight over a' the land is white—
Aw God! I'll up an' go to him a-singin' in the night,
      A-callin' in the night.

Grandmither, gie me your clay-cold heart that has forgot to ache
For mine be fire within my breast and yet it cannot break.

It beats an' throbs forever for the things that must not be,—
An' can ye not let me creep in an' rest awhile by ye?
A little lass afeard o' dark slept by ye years agone—
Ah, she has found what night can hold 'twixt sunset an' the dawn!
So when I plant the rose an' rue above your grave for ye,
Ye'll know it's under rue an' rose that I would like to be,
        That I would like to be.

A Likeness

Portrait Bust of an Unknown, Capitol, Rome

In every line a supple beauty—
    The restless head a little bent—
Disgust of pleasure, scorn of duty,
    The unseeing eyes of discontent.
I often come to sit beside him,
    This youth who passed and left no trace
Of good or ill that did betide him,
    Save the disdain upon his face.

The hope of all his House, the brother
    Adored, the golden-hearted son,
Whom Fortune pampered like a mother;
    And then—a shadow on the sun.
Whether he followed Cæsar's trumpet,
    Or chanced the riskier game at home
To find how favor played the strumpet
    In fickle politics at Rome;

Whether he dreamed a dream in Asia
    He never could forget by day,
Or gave his youth to some Aspasia,
    Or gamed his heritage away;
Once lost, across the Empire's border
    This man would seek his peace in vain;
His look arraigns a social order
    Somehow entrammelled with his pain.

"The dice of gods are always loaded";
    One gambler, arrogant as they,
Fierce, and by fierce injustice goaded,
    Left both his hazard and the play.

Incapable of compromises,
　Unable to forgive or spare,
The strange awarding of the prizes
　He had no fortitude to bear.

Tricked by the forms of things material—
　The solid-seeming arch and stone,
The noise of war, the pomp imperial,
　The heights and depths about a throne—
He missed, among the shapes diurnal,
　The old, deep-travelled road from pain,
The thoughts of men which are eternal,
　In which, eternal, men remain.

Ritratto d'ignoto; defying
　Things unsubstantial as a dream—
An Empire, long in ashes lying—
　His face still set against the stream.
Yes, so he looked, that gifted brother
　I loved, who passed and left no trace,
Not even—luckier than this other—
　His sorrow in a marble face.

JOSEPHINE PRESTON PEABODY (1874–1922)

Born in Brooklyn, New York, Josephine Preston Peabody first published one of her poems in *The Woman's Journal* when she was fourteen. She published poems in a few more magazines before the books, *The Wayfarers* (1898), *Fortune and Men's Eyes* (1900), and *Marlowe* (1901), a one-act play, appeared. Peabody was an English instructor at Wellesley College, and she married a Harvard engineering professor in 1906. *The Piper* (1909), a verse drama on the legend of the Pied Piper, won the Stratford Prize Competition and was performed at the Memorial Theatre in England. In addition to writing poetry for adults and children in the early twentieth century, Peabody also wrote dramas, including a play about Mary Wollstonecraft in 1922.

Prelude

Words, words,
Ye are like birds.
Would I might fold you,
In my hands hold you
Till ye were warm and your feathers a-flutter;
Till, in your throats,
Tremulous notes
Foretold the songs ye would utter.

Words, words,
Ye are all birds!
Would ye might linger
Here on my finger,
Till I kissed each, and then sent you a-winging
Wild, perfect flight,
Through morn to night,
Singing and singing and singing!

Rubric

I'll not believe the dullard dark,
Nor all the winds that weep,
But I shall find the farthest dream
That kisses me, asleep.

The Nightingale Unheard

Yes, Nightingale, through all the summer-time
　　We followed on, from moon to golden moon;
　　From where Salerno day-dreams in the noon,
And the far rose of Pæstum once did climb.
　　All the white way beside the girdling blue,
Through sun-shrill vines and campanile chime,
　　We listened;—from the old year to the new.
　　　　Brown bird, and where were you?

You, that Ravello lured not, throned on high
　　And filled with singing out of sun-burned throats!
　　Nor yet Minore of the flame-sailed boats;
Nor yet—of all bird-song should glorify—
　　Assisi, Little Portion of the blest,
Assisi, in the bosom of the sky,
　　Where God's own singer thatched his sunward nest.
　　　　That little, heavenliest!

And north and north, to where the hedge-rows are,
　　That beckon with white looks an endless way;
　　Where, through the fair wet silverness of May,
A lamb shines out as sudden as a star,
　　Among the cloudy sheep; and green, and pale,
The may-trees reach and glimmer, near or far,
　　And the red may-trees wear a shining veil.
　　　　And still, no nightingale!

The one vain longing,—through all journeyings,
　　The one: in every hushed and hearkening spot,—
　　All the soft-swarming dark where you were not,
Still longed for! Yes, for sake of dreams and wings,
　　And wonders, that your own must ever make
To bower you close, with all hearts' treasurings;
　　And for that speech toward which all hearts do ache;—
　　　　Even for Music's sake.

But most, his music whose belovèd name
　　Forever writ in water of bright tears,
　　Wins to one grave-side even the Roman years,
That kindle there the hallowed April flame
　　Of comfort-breathing violets. By that shrine
Of Youth, Love, Death, forevermore the same,

Violets still!—When falls, to leave no sign,
  The arch of Constantine.

Most for his sake we dreamed. Tho' not as he,
  From that lone spirit, brimmed with human woe
  Your song once shook to surging overflow.
How was it, sovran dweller of the tree,
  His cry, still throbbing in the flooded shell
Of silence with remembered melody,
  Could draw from you no answer to the spell?
    —O Voice, O Philomel?

Long time we wondered (and we knew not why):—
  Nor dream, nor prayer, of wayside gladness born,
  Nor vineyards waiting, nor reproachful thorn,
Nor yet the nested hill-towns set so high
  All the white way beside the girdling blue,—
Nor olives, gray against a golden sky,
  Could serve to wake that rapturous voice of you.
    But the wise silence knew.

O Nightingale unheard!—Unheard alone,
  Throughout that woven music of the days
  From the faint sea-rim to the market-place,
And ring of hammers on cathedral stone!
  So be it, better so: that there should fail
For sun-filled ones, one blessèd thing unknown.
  To them, be hid forever,—and all hail!
    Sing never, Nightingale.

Sing, for the others! Sing; to some pale cheek
  Against the window, like a starving flower.
  Loose, with your singing, one poor pilgrim hour
Of journey, with some Heart's Desire to seek.
  Loose, with your singing, captives such as these
In misery and iron, hearts too meek,
  For voyage—voyage over dreamful seas
    To lost Hesperides.

Sing not for free-men. Ah, but sing for whom
  The walls shut in; and even as eyes that fade,
  The windows take no heed of light nor shade,—
The leaves are lost in mutterings of the loom.
  Sing near! So in that golden overflowing

They may forget their wasted human bloom;
   Pay the devouring days their all, unknowing,—
     Reck not of life's bright going!

Sing not for lovers, side by side that hark;
   Nor unto parted lovers, save they be
   Parted indeed by more than makes the Sea,
Where never hope shall meet—like mounting lark—
   Far Joy's uprising; and no memories
Abide to star the music-haunted dark:
   To them that sit in darkness, such as these,
     Pour down, pour down heart's-ease.

Not in Kings' gardens. No; but where there haunt
   The world's forgotten, both of men and birds;
The alleys of no hope and of no words,
The hidings where men reap not, though they plant;
   But toil and thirst—so dying and so born;—
And toil and thirst to gather to their want,
   From the lean waste, beyond the daylight's scorn,
    —To gather grapes of thorn!

• • •

And for those two, your pilgrims without tears,
   Who prayed largess where there was no dearth,
Forgive it to their human-happy ears:
   Forgive it them, brown music of the Earth,
   Unknowing,—though the wiser silence knew!
Forgive it to the music of the spheres
   That while they walked together so, the Two
    Together,—heard not you.

AMY LOWELL (1874–1925)

Experimenting with free verse and polyphonic prose, Amy Lowell was the foremost American poet in the Imagist movement. The Massachusetts-born Lowell was educated in private schools. It wasn't until 1910 that she published her first poem in the *Atlantic Monthly*, and her first book, *A Dome of Many-Coloured Glass*, was published in 1912. In 1913, Lowell met Ezra Pound and the Imagists, and started trying out new forms of verse that veered away from traditional rhyming sequences. Some of her books of poetry are: *Sword Blades and Poppy Seed* (1914), *Men, Women, and Ghosts* (1916), and *Pictures of the Floating World* (1919). In addition to several more poetry books, Lowell also edited three Imagist anthologies. Of the sampling of poems that appear here, "Patterns" is her most famous.

The Letter

Little cramped words scrawling all over the paper
Like draggled fly's legs,
What can you tell of the flaring moon
Through the oak leaves?
Or of my uncurtained window and the bare floor
Spattered with moonlight?
Your silly quirks and twists have nothing in them
Of blossoming hawthorns,
And this paper is dull, crisp, smooth, virgin of loveliness
Beneath my hand.

I am tired, Beloved, of chafing my heart against
The want of you;
Of squeezing it into little inkdrops,
And posting it.
And I scald alone, here, under the fire
Of the great moon.

Venus Transiens

Tell me,
Was Venus more beautiful
Than you are,
When she topped
The crinkled waves,
Drifting shoreward
On her plaited shell?
Was Botticelli's vision

175

Fairer than mine;
And were the painted rosebuds
He tossed his lady,
Of better worth
Than the words I blow about you
To cover your too great loveliness
As with a gauze
Of misted silver?
For me,
You stand poised
In the blue and buoyant air,
Cinctured by bright winds,
Treading the sunlight.
And the waves which precede you
Ripple and stir
The sands at my feet.

The Garden by Moonlight

A black cat among roses,
Phlox, lilac-misted under a first-quarter moon,
The sweet smells of heliotrope and night-scented stock.
The garden is very still,
It is dazed with moonlight,
Contented with perfume,
Dreaming the opium dreams of its folded poppies.
Firefly lights open and vanish
High as the tip buds of the golden glow
Low as the sweet alyssum flowers at my feet.
Moon-shimmer on leaves and trellises,
Moon-spikes shafting through the snow-ball bush.
Only the little faces of the ladies' delight are alert and staring,
Only the cat, padding between the roses,
Shakes a branch and breaks the chequered pattern
As water is broken by the falling of a leaf.
Then you come,
And you are quiet like the garden,
And white like the alyssum flowers,
And beautiful as the silent sparks of the fireflies.
Ah, Beloved, do you see those orange lilies?
They knew my mother,

But who belonging to me will they know
When I am gone.

The Taxi

When I go away from you
The world beats dead
Like a slackened drum.
I call out for you against the jutted stars
And shout into the ridges of the wind.
Streets coming fast,
One after the other,
Wedge you away from me,
And the lamps of the city prick my eyes
So that I can no longer see your face.
Why should I leave you,
To wound myself upon the sharp edges of the night?

Patterns

I walk down the garden paths,
And all the daffodils
Are blowing, and the bright blue squills.
I walk down the patterned garden-paths
In my stiff, brocaded gown.
With my powdered hair and jewelled fan,
I too am a rare
Pattern. As I wander down
The garden paths.

My dress is richly figured,
And the train
Makes a pink and silver stain
On the gravel, and the thrift
Of the borders.
Just a plate of current fashion,
Tripping by in high-heeled, ribboned shoes.
Not a softness anywhere about me,
Only whalebone and brocade.
And I sink on a seat in the shade
Of a lime tree. For my passion
Wars against the stiff brocade.

The daffodils and squills
Flutter in the breeze
As they please.
And I weep;
For the lime-tree is in blossom
And one small flower has dropped upon my bosom.

And the plashing of waterdrops
In the marble fountain
Comes down the garden-paths.
The dripping never stops.
Underneath my stiffened gown
Is the softness of a woman bathing in a marble basin,
A basin in the midst of hedges grown
So thick, she cannot see her lover hiding,
But she guesses he is near,
And the sliding of the water
Seems the stroking of a dear
Hand upon her.
What is Summer in a fine brocaded gown!
I should like to see it lying in a heap upon the ground.
All the pink and silver crumpled up on the ground.

I would be the pink and silver as I ran along the paths,
And he would stumble after,
Bewildered by my laughter.
I should see the sun flashing from his sword-hilt and the buckles on his
    shoes.
I would choose
To lead him in a maze along the patterned paths,
A bright and laughing maze for my heavy-booted lover.
Till he caught me in the shade,
And the buttons of his waistcoat bruised my body as he clasped me,
Aching, melting, unafraid.
With the shadows of the leaves and the sundrops,
And the plopping of the waterdrops,
All about us in the open afternoon—
I am very like to swoon
With the weight of this brocade,
For the sun sifts through the shade.

Underneath the fallen blossom
In my bosom,

Is a letter I have hid.
It was brought to me this morning by a rider from the Duke.
"Madam, we regret to inform you that Lord Hartwell
Died in action Thursday se'nnight."
As I read it in the white, morning sunlight,
The letters squirmed like snakes.
"Any answer, Madam," said my footman.
"No," I told him.
"See that the messenger takes some refreshment.
No, no answer."
And I walked into the garden,
Up and down the patterned paths,
In my stiff, correct brocade.
The blue and yellow flowers stood up proudly in the sun,
Each one.
I stood upright too,
Held rigid to the pattern
By the stiffness of my gown.
Up and down I walked,
Up and down.

In a month he would have been my husband.
In a month, here, underneath this lime,
We would have broke the pattern;
He for me, and I for him,
He as Colonel, I as Lady,
On this shady seat.
He had a whim
That sunlight carried blessing.
And I answered, "It shall be as you have said."
Now he is dead.

In Summer and in Winter I shall walk
Up and down
The patterned garden-paths
In my stiff, brocaded gown.
The squills and daffodils
Will give place to pillared roses, and to asters, and to snow.
I shall go
Up and down,
In my gown.
Gorgeously arrayed,
Boned and stayed.

And the softness of my body will be guarded from embrace
By each button, hook, and lace.
For the man who should loose me is dead,
Fighting with the Duke in Flanders,
In a pattern called a war.
Christ! What are patterns for?

A Winter Ride

Who shall declare the joy of the running!
   Who shall tell of the pleasures of flight!
Springing and spurning the tufts of wild heather,
   Sweeping, wide-winged, through the blue dome of light.
Everything mortal has moments immortal,
   Swift and God-gifted, immeasurably bright.

So with the stretch of the white road before me,
   Shining snow crystals rainbowed by the sun,
Fields that are white, stained with long, cool, blue shadows,
   Strong with the strength of my horse as we run.
Joy in the touch of the wind and the sunlight!
   Joy! With the vigorous earth I am one.

Opal

You are ice and fire,
The touch of you burns my hands like snow.
You are cold and flame.
You are the crimson of amaryllis,
The silver of moon-touched magnolias.
When I am with you,
My heart is a frozen pond
Gleaming with agitated torches.

ALICE DUNBAR-NELSON (1875–1935)

Wife of poet Paul Laurence Dunbar, Alice Dunbar-Nelson was born in New Orleans, Louisiana. An advocate for African-American rights, Dunbar-Nelson was of mixed black, white, and Native American ancestry. She taught high school for twenty years, founded the Industrial School for Colored Girls in Delaware, and was active as a lecturer in the black women's club movement. She wrote *Violets*, a collection of stories, poems, and essays, and *The Goodness of St. Rocque*, short stories. She also edited *Masterpieces of Negro Eloquence*, speeches, and *The Dunbar Speaker and Entertainer*, a magazine. "I Sit and Sew," a war poem from 1920, reflects how powerless a woman feels while soldiers fight in the field.

Sonnet

I had no thought of violets of late,
The wild, shy kind that spring beneath your feet
In wistful April days, when lovers mate
And wander through the fields in raptures sweet.
The thought of violets meant florists' shops,
And bows and pins, and perfumed papers fine;
And garish lights, and mincing little fops
And cabarets and songs, and deadening wine.
So far from sweet real things my thoughts had strayed,
I had forgot wide fields, and clear brown streams;
The perfect loveliness that God has made,—
Wild violets shy and Heaven-mounting dreams.
And now—unwittingly, you've made me dream
Of violets, and my soul's forgotten gleam.

I Sit and Sew

I sit and sew—a useless task it seems,
My hands grown tired, my head weighed down with dreams—
The panoply of war, the martial tread of men,
Grim-faced, stern-eyed, gazing beyond the ken
Of lesser souls, whose eyes have not seen Death
Nor learned to hold their lives but as a breath—
But—I must sit and sew.

I sit and sew—my heart aches with desire—
That pageant terrible, that fiercely pouring fire
On wasted fields, and writhing grotesque things
Once men. My soul in pity flings

181

Appealing cries, yearning only to go
There in that holocaust of hell, those fields of woe—
But—I must sit and sew.

The little useless seam, the idle patch;
Why dream I here beneath my homely thatch,
When there they lie in sodden mud and rain,
Pitifully calling me, the quick ones and the slain?
You need me, Christ! It is no roseate dream
That beckons me—this pretty futile seam,
It stifles me—God, must I sit and sew?

ANNA HEMPSTEAD BRANCH (1875–1937)

Anna Hempstead Branch was born in New London, Connecticut, where her maternal family, the Hempsteads, had lived since 1640. Branch, whose father was a lawyer and mother a writer of children's stories and poems, was graduated from Smith College in 1897 and studied dramaturgy in New York. During her life, she worked for several social organizations and established the Poet's Guild, which was an association that helped make poetry more accessible to neighborhood children. Members of this association included Branch, Robert Frost, Edwin Arlington Robinson, Sara Teasdale, Carl Sandburg, and Vachel Lindsay, to name a few. Branch's long epic poem "Nimrod" is one of her better-known works. Her volumes include *The Shoes that Danced* (1905), *Rose of the Wind* (1910), and *Sonnets from a Lock Box* (1929).

Grieve Not, Ladies

Oh, grieve not, Ladies, if at night
    Ye wake to feel your beauty going.
It was a web of frail delight,
    Inconstant as an April snowing.

In other eyes, in other lands,
    In deep fair pools, new beauty lingers,
But like spent water in your hands
    It runs from your reluctant fingers.

Ye shall not keep the singing lark
    That owes to earlier skies its duty.
Weep not to hear along the dark
    The sound of your departing beauty.

The fine and anguished ear of night
    Is tuned to hear the smallest sorrow.
Oh, wait until the morning light!
    It may not seem so gone to-morrow!

But honey-pale and rosy-red!
    Brief lights that made a little shining!
Beautiful looks about us shed—
    They leave us to the old repining.

Think not the watchful dim despair
    Has come to you the first, sweet-hearted!
For oh, the gold in Helen's hair!
    And how she cried when that departed!

Perhaps that one that took the most,
   The swiftest borrower, wildest spender,
May count, as we would not, the cost—
   And grow more true to us and tender.

Happy are we if in his eyes
   We see no shadow of forgetting.
Nay—if our star sinks in those skies
   We shall not wholly see its setting.

Then let us laugh as do the brooks
   That such immortal youth is ours,
If memory keeps for them our looks
   As fresh as are the spring-time flowers.

Oh, grieve not, Ladies, if at night
   Ye wake, to feel the cold December!
Rather recall the early light
   And in your loved one's arms, remember.

Songs for My Mother

I

Her Hands

My mother's hands are cool and fair,
   They can do anything.
Delicate mercies hide them there
   Like flowers in the spring.

When I was small and could not sleep,
   She used to come to me,
And with my cheek upon her hand
   How sure my rest would be.

For everything she ever touched
   Of beautiful or fine,
Their memories living in her hands
   Would warm that sleep of mine.

Her hands remember how they played
   One time in meadow streams,—
And all the flickering song and shade
   Of water took my dreams.

Swift through her haunted fingers pass
   Memories of garden things;—
I dipped my face in flowers and grass
   And sounds of hidden wings.

One time she touched the cloud that kissed
   Brown pastures bleak and far;—
I leaned my cheek into a mist
   And thought I was a star.

All this was very long ago
   And I am grown; but yet
The hand that lured my slumber so
   I never can forget.

For still when drowsiness comes on
   It seems so soft and cool,
Shaped happily beneath my cheek,
   Hollow and beautiful.

II

Her Words

My mother has the prettiest tricks
   Of words and words and words.
Her talk comes out as smooth and sleek
   As breasts of singing birds.

She shapes her speech all silver fine
   Because she loves it so.
And her own eyes begin to shine
   To hear her stories grow.

And if she goes to make a call
   Or out to take a walk
We leave our work when she returns
   And run to hear her talk.

We had not dreamed these things were so
   Of sorrow and of mirth.
Her speech is as a thousand eyes
   Through which we see the earth.

God wove a web of loveliness,
   Of clouds and stars and birds,

But made not any thing at all
  So beautiful as words.

They shine around our simple earth
  With golden shadowings,
And every common thing they touch
  Is exquisite with wings.

There's nothing poor and nothing small
  But is made fair with them.
They are the hands of living faith
  That touch the garment's hem.

They are as fair as bloom or air,
  They shine like any star,
And I am rich who learned from her
  How beautiful they are.

SARA TEASDALE (1884-1933)

Born in St. Louis, Missouri, Sara Teasdale contributed some sonnets to the privately printed literary monthly, the *Wheel*. Her first book, *Sonnets to Duse, and Other Poems* (1907), was followed by *Helen of Troy, and Other Poems* (1911), and *Rivers to the Sea* (1915). Teasdale married a businessman, whom she later divorced in 1929, and moved to New York. In 1918, Teasdale won both the Pulitzer Prize for poetry and the annual Poetry Society of America prize for *Love Songs* (1917). She also edited an anthology of poems for children and another composed of love poems written by women. Her later books such as *Flame and Shadow* (1920) and *Dark of the Moon* (1926) are enriched with more maturity and passion than her earlier works. While working on a biography of English poet Christina Rossetti, Teasdale fell ill with pneumonia, overdosed on barbiturates and died in January, 1933.

Barter

Life has loveliness to sell,
  All beautiful and splendid things,
Blue waves whitened on a cliff,
  Soaring fire that sways and sings,
And children's faces looking up
Holding wonder like a cup.

Life has loveliness to sell,
  Music like a curve of gold,
Scent of pine trees in the rain,
  Eyes that love you, arms that hold,
And for your spirit's still delight,
Holy thoughts that star the night.

Spend all you have for loveliness,
  Buy it and never count the cost;
For one white singing hour of peace
  Count many a year of strife well lost,
And for a breath of ecstasy
Give all you have been, or could be.

The Look

Strephon kissed me in the spring,
  Robin in the fall,
But Colin only looked at me
  And never kissed at all.

187

Strephon's kiss was lost in jest,
   Robin's lost in play,
But the kiss in Colin's eyes
   Haunts me night and day.

The Kiss

I hoped that he would love me,
   And he has kissed my mouth,
But I am like a stricken bird
   That cannot reach the south.

For though I know he loves me,
   To-night my heart is sad;
His kiss was not so wonderful
   As all the dreams I had.

I Shall Not Care

When I am dead and over me bright April
   Shakes out her rain-drenched hair,
Though you should lean above me broken-hearted,
   I shall not care.

I shall have peace as leafy trees are peaceful,
   When rain bends down the bough,
And I shall be more silent and cold-hearted
   Than you are now.

The Wind

A tall tree talking with the wind
   Leans as he leaned to me—
But oh the wind waits where she will,
   The wind is free.

I am a woman, I am weak,
   And custom leads me as one blind,
Only my songs go where they will
   Free as the wind.

The Answer

When I go back to earth
And all my joyous body
Puts off the red and white
That once had been so proud,
If men should pass above
With false and feeble pity,
My dust will find a voice
To answer them aloud:

"Be still, I am content,
Take back your poor compassion,
Joy was a flame in me
Too steady to destroy;
Lithe as a bending reed
Loving the storm that sways her—
I found more joy in sorrow
Than you could find in joy."

Appraisal

Never think she loves him wholly,
Never believe her love is blind,
All his faults are locked securely
In a closet of her mind;
All his indecisions folded
Like old flags that time has faded,
Limp and streaked with rain,
And his cautiousness like garments
Frayed and thin, with many a stain—
Let them be, oh let them be,
There is treasure to outweigh them,
His proud will that sharply stirred,
Climbs as surely as the tide,
Senses strained too taut to sleep,
Gentleness to beast and bird,
Humor flickering hushed and wide
As the moon on moving water,
And a tenderness too deep
To be gathered in a word.

The Solitary

My heart has grown rich with the passing of years,
 I have less need now than when I was young
To share myself with every comer
 Or shape my thoughts into words with my tongue.

It is one to me that they come or go
 If I have myself and the drive of my will,
And strength to climb on a summer night
 And watch the stars swarm over the hill.

Let them think I love them more than I do,
 Let them think I care, though I go alone;
If it lifts their pride, what is it to me
 Who am self-complete as a flower or a stone.

Sappho

The twilight's inner flame grows blue and deep,
And in my Lesbos, over leagues of sea,
The temples glimmer moonwise in the trees.
Twilight has veiled the little flower face
Here on my heart, but still the night is kind
And leaves her warm sweet weight against my breast.
Am I that Sappho who would run at dusk
Along the surges creeping up the shore
When tides came in to ease the hungry beach,
And running, running, till the night was black,
Would fall forespent upon the chilly sand
And quiver with the winds from off the sea?
Ah, quietly the shingle waits the tides
Whose waves are stinging kisses, but to me
Love brought no peace, nor darkness any rest.
I crept and touched the foam with fevered hands
And cried to Love, from whom the sea is sweet,
From whom the sea is bitterer than death.
Ah, Aphrodite, if I sing no more
To thee, God's daughter, powerful as God,
It is that thou hast made my life too sweet
To hold the added sweetness of a song.
There is a quiet at the heart of love,

And I have pierced the pain and come to peace.
I hold my peace, my Cleïs, on my heart;
And softer than a little wild bird's wing
Are kisses that she pours upon my mouth.
Ah, never any more when spring like fire
Will flicker in the newly opened leaves,
Shall I steal forth to seek for solitude
Beyond the lure of light Alcæus' lyre,
Beyond the sob that stilled Erinna's voice.
Ah, never with a throat that aches with song,
Beneath the white uncaring sky of spring,
Shall I go forth to hide awhile from Love
The quiver and the crying of my heart.
Still I remember how I strove to flee
The love-note of the birds, and bowed my head
To hurry faster, but upon the ground
I saw two wingèd shadows side by side,
And all the world's spring passion stifled me.
Ah, Love, there is no fleeing from thy might,
No lonely place where thou hast never trod,
No desert thou hast left uncarpeted
With flowers that spring beneath thy perfect feet.
In many guises didst thou come to me;
I saw thee by the maidens while they danced,
Phaon allured me with a look of thine,
In Anactoria I knew thy grace,
I looked at Cercolas and saw thine eyes;
But never wholly, soul and body mine,
Didst thou bid any love me as I loved.
Now I have found the peace that fled from me;
Close, close, against my heart I hold my world.
Ah, Love that made my life a lyric cry,
Ah, Love that tuned my lips to lyres of thine,
I taught the world thy music, now alone
I sing for one who falls asleep to hear.

ELINOR WYLIE (1885–1928)

Born in Somerville, New Jersey, Elinor Wylie attended private schools in Washington, D.C., where her father was assistant U.S. attorney general. She caused a social upheaval in 1910 when she left her first husband for Horace Wylie, a lawyer seventeen years her senior. In 1912, Wylie's mother published an anonymous volume of her daughter's poems. Appearing under her own name, *Nets to Catch the Wind* (1921) was praised by both the critics and the public. Following her book's success, Wylie moved to New York City and hobnobbed with the literary society there. She continued to write poetry for magazines and married her third husband, William Rose Benét, in 1923. Her subsequent books include: *Black Armour* (1923), *Jennifer Lorn* (1923), one of four novels, and *Angels and Earthly Creatures* (1929). Her *Collected Poems* (1932) and *Collected Prose* (1933), both edited by Benét, were published posthumously.

Beauty

Say not of Beauty she is good,
Or aught but beautiful,
Or sleek to doves' wings of the wood
Her wild wings of a gull.

Call her not wicked; that word's touch
Consumes her like a curse;
But love her not too much, too much,
For that is even worse.

O, she is neither good nor bad,
But innocent and wild!
Enshrine her and she dies, who had
The hard heart of a child.

The Eagle and the Mole

Avoid the reeking herd,
Shun the polluted flock,
Live like that stoic bird,
The eagle of the rock.

The huddled warmth of crowds
Begets and fosters hate;
He keeps, above the clouds,
His cliff inviolate.

When flocks are folded warm,
And herds to shelter run,
He sails above the storm,
He stares into the sun,

If in the eagle's track
Your sinews cannot leap,
Avoid the lathered pack,
Turn from the steaming sheep.

If you would keep your soul
From spotted sight or sound,
Live like the velvet mole;
Go burrow underground.

And there hold intercourse
With roots of trees and stones,
With rivers at their source,
And disembodied bones.

Velvet Shoes

Let us walk in the white snow
   In a soundless space;
With footsteps quiet and slow,
   At a tranquil pace,
   Under veils of white lace.

I shall go shod in silk,
   And you in wool,
White as a white cow's milk,
   More beautiful
   Than the breast of a gull.

We shall walk through the still town
   In a windless peace;
We shall step upon white down,
   Upon silver fleece,
   Upon softer than these.

We shall walk in velvet shoes:
   Wherever we go
Silence will fall like dews
   On white silence below.
   We shall walk in the snow.

Let No Charitable Hope

Now let no charitable hope
Confuse my mind with images
Of eagle and of antelope:
I am in nature none of these.

I was, being human, born alone;
I am, being woman, hard beset;
I live by squeezing from a stone
The little nourishment I get.

In masks outrageous and austere
The years go by in single file;
But none has merited my fear,
And none has quite escaped my smile.

Pretty Words

Poets make pets of pretty, docile words:
I love smooth words, like gold-enameled fish
Which circle slowly with a silken swish,
And tender ones, like downy-feathered birds:
Words shy and dappled, deep-eyed deer in herds,
Come to my hand, and playful if I wish,
Or purring softly at a silver dish,
Blue Persian kittens, fed on cream and curds.

I love bright words, words up and singing early;
Words that are luminous in the dark, and sing;
Warm lazy words, white cattle under trees;
I love words opalescent, cool, and pearly,
Like midsummer moths, and honied words like bees,
Gilded and sticky, with a little sting.

HAZEL HALL (1886–1924)

Born in St. Paul, Minnesota, Hazel Hall began writing verse when she was thirty years old. Raised in Portland, Oregon, she was paralyzed at the age of twelve and confined to a wheelchair for the remainder of her life. Hall's poems and her needlework became her livelihood. She published *Curtains* (1922), *Walkers* (1923), and *Cry of Time* (1928, published posthumously).

White Branches

I had forgotten the gesture of branches
Suddenly white,
And I had forgotten the fragrance of blossoms
Filling a room at night.

In remembering the curve of branches
Who beckoned me in vain,
Remembering dark rooms of coolness
Where fragrance was like pain,
I have forgotten all else; there is nothing
That signifies—
There is only the brush of branch and white breath
Against my lips and eyes.

Instruction

My hands that guide a needle
   In their turn are led
Relentlessly and deftly,
   As a needle leads a thread.

Other hands are teaching
   My needle; when I sew
I feel the cool, thin fingers
   Of hands I do not know.

They urge my needle onward,
   They smooth my seams, until
The worry of my stitches
   Smothers in their skill.

All the tired women,
   Who sewed their lives away,
Speak in my deft fingers
   As I sew today.

HILDA DOOLITTLE (1886–1961)

While attending Bryn Mawr College, Hilda Doolittle met fellow poets Marianne Moore, Ezra Pound, and William Carlos Williams. In 1911, Doolittle traveled to Europe and eventually made her home there. Ezra Pound, pivotal in the development of Imagism, encouraged her to submit her poetry to Harriet Monroe's magazine, *Poetry*. Her early poems were published with the pseudonym "H. D." in periodicals such as London's *The Egoist*, edited by Richard Aldington, who became her husband in 1913. Doolittle emerged as one of the newer Imagist poets with her first volume of poems, *Sea Garden* (1916). Her other books include: *Hymen* (1921), *Heliodora and Other Poems* (1924), *Red Roses for Bronze* (1931), and various prose works, including four novels. In 1960, Doolittle received the Award of Merit Medal for poetry.

Oread

Whirl up, sea—
whirl your pointed pines,
splash your great pines
on our rocks,
hurl your green over us,
cover us with your pools of fir.

Sea Poppies

Amber husk
fluted with gold,
fruit on the sand
marked with a rich grain,

treasure
spilled near the shrub-pines
to bleach on the boulders:

your stalk has caught root
among wet pebbles
and drift flung by the sea
and grated shells
and split conch-shells.

Beautiful, wide-spread,
fire upon leaf,
what meadow yields
so fragrant a leaf
as your bright leaf?

Sheltered Garden

I have had enough.
I gasp for breath.

Every way ends, every road,
every foot-path leads at last
to the hill-crest—
then you retrace your steps,
or find the same slope on the other side,
precipitate.

I have had enough—
border-pinks, clove-pinks, wax-lilies,
herbs, sweet-cress.

O for some sharp swish of a branch—
there is no scent of resin
in this place,
no taste of bark, of coarse weeds,
aromatic, astringent—
only border on border of scented pinks.

Have you seen fruit under cover
that wanted light—
pears wadded in cloth,
protected from the frost,
melons, almost ripe,
smothered in straw?

Why not let the pears cling
to the empty branch?
All your coaxing will only make
a bitter fruit—
let them cling, ripen of themselves,
test their own worth,
nipped, shrivelled by the frost,
to fall at last but fair
with a russet coat.

Or the melon—
let it bleach yellow
in the winter light,
even tart to the taste—
it is better to taste of frost—

the exquisite frost—
than of wadding and of dead grass.

For this beauty,
beauty without strength,
chokes out life.
I want wind to break,
scatter these pink-stalks,
snap off their spiced heads,
fling them about with dead leaves—
spread the paths with twigs,
limbs broken off,
trail great pine branches,
hurled from some far wood
right across the melon-patch,
break pear and quince—
leave half-trees, torn, twisted
but showing the fight was valiant.

O to blot out this garden
to forget, to find a new beauty
in some terrible
wind-tortured place.

Heat

O wind, rend open the heat,
cut apart the heat,
rend it to tatters.

Fruit cannot drop
through this thick air—
fruit cannot fall into heat
that presses up and blunts
the points of pears
and rounds the grapes.

Cut the heat—
plough through it,
turning it on either side
of your path.

Helen

All Greece hates
the still eyes in the white face,
the lustre as of olives
where she stands,
and the white hands.

All Greece reviles
the wan face when she smiles,
hating it deeper still
when it grows wan and white,
remembering past enchantments
and past ills.

Greece sees unmoved,
God's daughter, born of love,
the beauty of cool feet
and slenderest knees,
could love indeed the maid,
only if she were laid,
white ash amid funereal cypresses.

GEORGIA DOUGLAS JOHNSON (1886–1966)

The first African-American woman poet to become famous since Frances E. W. Harper, Georgia Douglas Johnson was born in Atlanta, Georgia, and educated in public schools. Her emotional style is evident in her three books: *The Heart of a Woman* (1918), *Bronze* (1922), and *An Autumn Love Cycle* (1928).

The Heart of a Woman

The heart of a woman goes forth with the dawn,
As a lone bird, soft winging, so restlessly on,
Afar o'er life's turrets and vales does it roam
In the wake of those echoes the heart calls home.

The heart of a woman falls back with the night,
And enters some alien cage in its plight,
And tries to forget it has dreamed of the stars,
While it breaks, breaks, breaks on the sheltering bars.

MARIANNE MOORE (1887–1972)

Characterized by a highly personal and unique style, Marianne Moore's verse has earned a distinctive place in twentieth-century American poetry. Born in St. Louis, Missouri, Moore taught school after graduating from Bryn Mawr College in 1909. She worked as an assistant librarian in the New York Public Library during 1921–25. Without her knowledge, *Poems* (1921) was published, edited by Hilda Doolittle and Winifred Ellerman. Moore's verse also appeared in various magazines and periodicals, as well as in *Selected Poems* (1935), *The Pangolin and Other Poems* (1936), *What Are Years* (1941), and *Collected Poems* (1951), which won her a Pulitzer Prize plus two additional awards.

Poetry

I, too, dislike it: there are things that are important beyond all this
    fiddle.
  Reading it, however, with a perfect contempt for it, one discovers in
  it after all, a place for the genuine.
      Hands that can grasp, eyes
      that can dilate, hair that can rise
        if it must, these things are important not because a

high-sounding interpretation can be put upon them but because they
    are
  useful. When they become so derivative as to become unintelligible,
  the same things may be said for all of us, that we
      do not admire what
      we cannot understand: the bat
        holding on upside down or in quest of something to

eat, elephants pushing, a wild horse taking a roll, a tireless wolf under
    a tree, the immovable critic twitching his skin like a horse that feels a
    flea, the base-
  ball fan, the statistician—
  nor is it valid
      to discriminate against 'business documents and

school-books'; all these phenomena are important. One must make a
    distinction
  however: when dragged into prominence by half poets, the result is
    not poetry,
  nor till the poets among us can be

'literalists of
the imagination'—above
insolence and triviality and can present

for inspection, 'imaginary gardens with real toads in them', shall we
have
it. In the meantime, if you demand on the one hand,
the raw material of poetry in
all its rawness and
that which is on the other hand
genuine, you are interested in poetry.

Sojourn in the Whale

Trying to open locked doors with a sword, threading
The points of needles, planting shade trees
Upside down; swallowed by the opaqueness of one whom the seas
Love better than they love you, Ireland—

You have lived and lived on every kind of shortage.
You have been compelled by hags to spin
Gold thread from straw and have heard men say: "There is a feminine
Temperament in direct contrast to

Ours which makes her do these things. Circumscribed by a
Heritage of blindness and native
Incompetence, she will become wise and will be forced to give
In. Compelled by experience, she

Will turn back; water seeks its own level": and you
Have smiled. "Water in motion is far
From level." You have seen it when obstacles happened to bar
The path—rise automatically.

Roses Only

You do not seem to realize that beauty is a liability rather than
An asset—that in view of the fact that spirit creates form—we are jus-
tified in supposing
That you must have brains. For you, a symbol of the unit, stiff and
sharp,
Conscious of surpassing—by dint of native superiority and liking for
everything
Self dependent—anything an

Ambitious civilization might produce: for you, unaided to attempt through sheer
  Reserve, to confute presumptions resulting from observation, is idle. You cannot make us
    Think you a delightful happen-so. But rose, if you are brilliant, it
Is not because your petals are the without-which-nothing of pre-eminence. You would look—minus
Thorns—like a what-is-this, a mere

Peculiarity. They are not proof against a worm, the elements, or mildew
  But what about the predatory hand? What is brilliance without co-ordination? Guarding the
    Infinitesmal pieces of your mind, compelling audience to
  The remark that is better to be forgotten than to be remembered too violently,
Your thorns are the best part of you.

To a Steam Roller

The illustration
  Is nothing to you without the application.
  You lack half wit. You crush all the particles down
    Into close conformity and then walk back and forth on them.

Sparkling chips of rock
Are crushed down to the level of the parent block.
  Were not "impersonal judgment in aesthetic
    Matters, a metaphysical impossibility," you

Might fairly achieve
It. As for butterflies, I can hardly conceive
  Of one's attending upon you, but to question
    The congruence of the complement is vain, if it exists.

EDNA ST. VINCENT MILLAY (1892–1950)

Famous for her lyrical and passionate sonnets, Edna St. Vincent Millay was born in Rockland, Maine, and attended Vassar, graduating in 1917. At nineteen, Millay's poem "Renascence" was published in *The Lyric Year* (1912). She lived in New York's Greenwich Village, and was associated with the youthful, bohemian lifestyle prevalent there in the 1920s. *Renascence and Other Poems* (1917) was her first book of verse. In 1920, she published her second book of poems, *A Few Figs from Thistles*, and the following year, *Second April* appeared, along with two plays, *Two Slatterns and a King* and *The Lamp and the Bell*. She received the Pulitzer Prize in 1923 for her book, *Ballad of the Harp-Weaver*. That same year, Millay married a Dutch businessman and moved to Austerlitz, New York, where she died in 1950.

First Fig

My candle burns at both ends;
   It will not last the night;
But ah, my foes and oh, my friends—
   It gives a lovely light.

Renascence

All I could see from where I stood
Was three long mountains and a wood;
I turned and looked another way,
And saw three islands in a bay.
So with my eyes I traced the line
Of the horizon, thin and fine,
Straight around till I was come
Back to where I'd started from;
And all I saw from where I stood
Was three long mountains and a wood.
Over these things I could not see;
These were the things that bounded me;
And I could touch them with my hand,
Almost, I thought, from where I stand.
And all at once things seemed so small
My breath came short, and scarce at all.
But, sure, the sky is big, I said;
Miles and miles above my head;
So here upon my back I'll lie
And look my fill into the sky.
And so I looked, and, after all,

The sky was not so very tall.
The sky, I said, must somewhere stop,
And—sure enough!—I see the top!
The sky, I thought, is not so grand;
I 'most could touch it with my hand!
And reaching up my hand to try,
I screamed to feel it touch the sky.
I screamed, and—lo!—Infinity
Came down and settled over me;
Forced back my scream into my chest,
Bent back my arm upon my breast,
And, pressing of the Undefined
The definition on my mind,
Held up before my eyes a glass
Through which my shrinking sight did pass
Until it seemed I must behold
Immensity made manifold;
Whispered to me a word whose sound
Deafened the air for worlds around,
And brought unmuffled to my ears
The gossiping of friendly spheres,
The creaking of the tented sky,
The ticking of Eternity.
I saw and heard, and knew at last
The How and Why of all things, past,
And present, and forevermore.
The Universe, cleft to the core,
Lay open to my probing sense
That, sick'ning, I would fain pluck thence
But could not,—nay! But needs must suck
At the great wound, and could not pluck
My lips away till I had drawn
All venom out.—Ah, fearful pawn!
For my omniscience paid I toll
In infinite remorse of soul.
All sin was of my sinning, all
Atoning mine, and mine the gall
Of all regret. Mine was the weight
Of every brooded wrong, the hate
That stood behind each envious thrust,
Mine every greed, mine every lust.

And all the while for every grief,
Each suffering, I craved relief
With individual desire,—
Craved all in vain! And felt fierce fire
About a thousand people crawl;
Perished with each,—then mourned for all!
A man was starving in Capri;
He moved his eyes and looked at me;
I felt his gaze, I heard his moan,
And knew his hunger as my own.
I saw at sea a great fog bank
Between two ships that struck and sank;
A thousand screams the heavens smote;
And every scream tore through my throat.
No hurt I did not feel, no death
That was not mine; mine each last breath
That, crying, met an answering cry
From the compassion that was I.
All suffering mine, and mine its rod;
Mine, pity like the pity of God.
Ah, awful weight! Infinity
Pressed down upon the finite Me!
My anguished spirit, like a bird,
Beating against my lips I heard;
Yet lay the weight so close about
There was no room for it without.
And so beneath the weight lay I
And suffered death, but could not die.

Long had I lain thus, craving death,
When quietly the earth beneath
Gave way, and inch by inch, so great
At last had grown the crushing weight,
Into the earth I sank till I
Full six feet under ground did lie,
And sank no more,—there is no weight
Can follow here, however great.
From off my breast I felt it roll,
And as it went my tortured soul
Burst forth and fled in such a gust
That all about me swirled the dust.

Deep in the earth I rested now;
Cool is its hand upon the brow
And soft its breast beneath the head
Of one who is so gladly dead.
And all at once, and over all
The pitying rain began to fall;
I lay and heard each pattering hoof
Upon my lowly, thatchèd roof,
And seemed to love the sound far more
Than ever I had done before.
For rain it hath a friendly sound
To one who's six feet underground;
And scarce the friendly voice or face:
A grave is such a quiet place.

The rain, I said, is kind to come
And speak to me in my new home.
I would I were alive again
To kiss the fingers of the rain,
To drink into my eyes the shine
Of every slanting silver line,
To catch the freshened, fragrant breeze
From drenched and dripping apple-trees.
For soon the shower will be done,
And then the broad face of the sun
Will laugh above the rain-soaked earth
Until the world with answering mirth
Shakes joyously, and each round drop
Rolls, twinkling, from its grass-blade top.
How can I bear it; buried here,
While overhead the sky grows clear
And blue again after the storm?
O, multi-colored, multiform,
Beloved beauty over me,
That I shall never, never see
Again! Spring-silver, autumn-gold,
That I shall never more behold!
Sleeping your myriad magics through,
Close-sepulchred away from you!
O God, I cried, give me new birth,
And put me back upon the earth!

Upset each cloud's gigantic gourd
And let the heavy rain, down-poured
In one big torrent, set me free,
Washing my grave away from me!

I ceased; and through the breathless hush
That answered me, the far-off rush
Of herald wings came whispering
Like music down the vibrant string
Of my ascending prayer, and—crash!
Before the wild wind's whistling lash
The startled storm-clouds reared on high
And plunged in terror down the sky,
And the big rain in one black wave
Fell from the sky and struck my grave.
I know not how such things can be;
I only know there came to me
A fragrance such as never clings
To aught save happy living things;
A sound as of some joyous elf
Singing sweet songs to please himself,
And, through and over everything,
A sense of glad awakening.
The grass, a-tiptoe at my ear,
Whispering to me I could hear;
I felt the rain's cool finger-tips
Brushed tenderly across my lips,
Laid gently on my sealèd sight,
And all at once the heavy night
Fell from my eyes and I could see,—
A drenched and dripping apple-tree,
A last long line of silver rain,
A sky grown clear and blue again.
And as I looked a quickening gust
Of wind blew up to me and thrust
Into my face a miracle
Of orchard-breath, and with the smell,—
I know not how such things can be!—
I breathed my soul back into me.
Ah! Up then from the ground sprang I
And hailed the earth with such a cry
As is not heard save from a man

Who has been dead, and lives again.
About the trees my arms I wound;
Like one gone mad I hugged the ground;
I raised my quivering arms on high;
I laughed and laughed into the sky,
Till at my throat a strangling sob
Caught fiercely, and a great heart-throb
Sent instant tears into my eyes;
O God, I cried, no dark disguise
Can e'er hereafter hide from me
Thy radiant identity!
Thou canst not move across the grass
But my quick eyes will see Thee pass,
Nor speak, however silently,
But my hushed voice will answer Thee.
I know the path that tells Thy way
Through the cool eve of every day;
God, I can push the grass apart
And lay my finger on Thy heart!

The world stands out on either side
No wider than the heart is wide;
Above the world is stretched the sky,—
No higher than the soul is high.
The heart can push the sea and land
Farther away on either hand;
The soul can split the sky in two,
And let the face of God shine through.
But East and West will pinch the heart
That can not keep them pushed apart;
And he whose soul is flat—the sky
Will cave in on him by and by.

God's World

O world, I cannot hold thee close enough!
    Thy winds, thy wide grey skies!
    Thy mists, that roll and rise!
Thy woods, this autumn day, that ache and sag
And all but cry with colour! That gaunt crag
To crush! To lift the lean of that black bluff!
World, World, I cannot get thee close enough!

Long have I known a glory in it all,
　　But never knew I this;
　　Here such a passion is
As stretcheth me apart,—Lord, I do fear
Thou'st made the world too beautiful this year;
My soul is all but out of me,—let fall
No burning leaf; prithee, let no bird call.

Wild Swans

I looked in my heart while the wild swans went over.
And what did I see I had not seen before?
Only a question less or a question more;
Nothing to match the flight of wild birds flying.
Tiresome heart, forever living and dying,
House without air, I leave you and lock your door.
Wild swans, come over the town, come over
The town again, trailing your legs and crying!

Pity Me Not

Pity me not because the light of day
At close of day no longer walks the sky;
Pity me not for beauties passed away
From field and thicket as the year goes by;
Pity me not the waning of the moon,
Nor that the ebbing tide goes out to sea,
Nor that a man's desire is hushed so soon,
And you no longer look with love on me.

This have I known always: love is no more
Than the wide blossom which the wind assails;
Than the great tide that treads the shifting shore,
Strewing fresh wreckage gathered in the gales.
Pity me that the heart is slow to learn
What the swift mind beholds at every turn.

"Into the golden vessel of great song"

Into the golden vessel of great song
Let us pour all our passion; breast to breast
Let other lovers lie, in love and rest;
Not we,—articulate, so, but with the tongue
Of all the world: the churning blood, the long
Shuddering quiet, the desperate hot palms pressed
Sharply together upon the escaping guest,
The common soul, unguarded, and grown strong.
Longing alone is singer to the lute;
Let still on nettles in the open sigh
The minstrel, that in slumber is as mute
As any man, and love be far and high,
That else forsakes the topmost branch, a fruit
Found on the ground by every passer-by.

"I, being born a woman and distressed"

I, being born a woman and distressed
By all the needs and notions of my kind,
Am urged by your propinquity to find
Your person fair, and feel a certain zest
To bear your body's weight upon my breast:
So subtly is the fume of life designed,
To clarify the pulse and cloud the mind,
And leave me once again undone, possessed.
Think not for this, however, the poor treason
Of my stout blood against my staggering brain,
I shall remember you with love, or season
My scorn with pity,—let me make it plain:
I find this frenzy insufficient reason
For conversation when we meet again.

"Euclid alone has looked on Beauty bare"

Euclid alone has looked on Beauty bare.
Let all who prate of Beauty hold their peace,
And lay them prone upon the earth and cease
To ponder on themselves, the while they stare
At nothing, intricately drawn nowhere
In shapes of shifting lineage; let geese
Gabble and hiss, but heroes seek release
From dusty bondage into luminous air.
O blinding hour, O holy, terrible day,
When first the shaft into his vision shone
Of light anatomized! Euclid alone
Has looked on Beauty bare. Fortunate they
Who, though once only and then but far away,
Have heard her massive sandal set on stone.

"What lips my lips have kissed, and where, and why"

What lips my lips have kissed, and where, and why,
I have forgotten, and what arms have lain
Under my head till morning; but the rain
Is full of ghosts to-night, that tap and sigh
Upon the glass and listen for reply,
And in my heart there stirs a quiet pain
For unremembered lads that not again
Will turn to me at midnight with a cry.
Thus in the winter stands the lonely tree,
Nor knows what birds have vanished one by one,
Yet knows its boughs more silent than before:
I cannot say what loves have come and gone,
I only know that summer sang in me
A little while, that in me sings no more.

DOROTHY PARKER (1893–1967)

Born in West End, New Jersey, author Dorothy Parker joined the staff of *Vogue* in 1916 before working at *Vanity Fair* in 1917. Her first book of witty verse, *Enough Rope*, was published in 1926 and became a best-seller. She worked as a book reviewer for *The New Yorker* in 1927 and continued writing for the magazine for the rest of her career. Parker, famous for her quips, was a talented conversationalist, and soon came to represent the liberated woman of the twenties. Her later poems were published in *Sunset Gun* (1928), *Death and Taxes* (1931), and *Collected Poems: Not So Deep as a Well* (1936). Parker was married twice, and collaborated on film scenarios and a play. She died in New York City on June 7, 1967.

One Perfect Rose

A single flow'r he sent me, since we met.
　　All tenderly his messenger he chose;
Deep-hearted, pure, with scented dew still wet—
　　One perfect rose.

I knew the language of the floweret;
　　"My fragile leaves," it said, "his heart enclose."
Love long has taken for his amulet
　　One perfect rose.

Why is it no one ever sent me yet
　　One perfect limousine, do you suppose?
Ah no, it's always just my luck to get
　　One perfect rose.

Unfortunate Coincidence

By the time you swear you're his,
　　Shivering and sighing,
And he vows his passion is
　　Infinite, undying—
Lady, make a note of this:
　　One of you is lying.

GENEVIEVE TAGGARD (1894–1948)

Born in Waitsburg, Washington, Genevieve Taggard was raised in Hawaii. Her first published poem appeared in the *Oahuan*, and she was editor of the magazine four years later. She moved to New York City in 1920 and edited *The Measure*, a monthly poetry magazine. She frequently contributed to such periodicals as the *Freeman*, the *Masses*, and the *Liberator*. *For Eager Lovers* (1922), her first volume of verse, was highly praised. It was followed by *Hawaiian Hilltop* (1923), *May Days* (1925), a poetry anthology, and *Words for the Chisel* (1926). Taggard also taught English at Mount Holyoke College in 1929–30, published a biography of Emily Dickinson, and wrote song lyrics for composers like Aaron Copland. She was married twice and was awarded a Guggenheim Fellowship in 1931.

For Eager Lovers

I understand what you were running for,
Slim naked boy, and why from far inland
You came between dark hills. I know the roar
The sea makes in some ears. I understand.

I understand why you were running now,
And how you heard the sea resound, and how
You leaped and left your valley for the long
Brown road. I understand the song

You chanted with your running, with your feet
Marking the measure of your high heart's beat.
Now you are broken. Seeing your wide brow,
I see your dreams. I understand you now.

Since I have run like you, I understand
The throat's long wish, the breath that comes so quick,
The heart's light leap, the heels that drag so sick,
And warped heat wrinkles, lengthening the sand. . . .

Now you are broken. Seeing your wide brow
I see your dreams, understanding now
The cry, the certainty, wide arms—and then
The way rude ocean rises and descends. . . .

I saw you stretched and wounded where tide ends.
I do not want to walk that way again.

LOUISE BOGAN (1897–1970)

Louise Bogan, born in Livermore Falls, Maine, left Boston University after her marriage in 1916. Widowed with a young child four years later, Bogan first published her poems in *The New Republic* as well as in *Poetry* and the *Atlantic Monthly*. Her books include *Body of This Death* (1923), *Dark Summer* (1929), *Collected Poems* (1954), and *The Blue Estuaries: Poems 1923–1968*. Bogan also wrote two books of poetry criticism and was poetry critic for *The New Yorker*. She won many prizes, including two from *Poetry* magazine and a National Endowment for the Arts award in 1967. Bogan frequently lectured at various colleges and universities and was elected to the American Academy of Arts and Letters.

Medusa

I had come to the house, in a cave of trees,
Facing a sheer sky.
Everything moved,—a bell hung ready to strike,
Sun and reflection wheeled by.

When the bare eyes were before me
And the hissing hair,
Held up at a window, seen through a door.
The stiff bald eyes, the serpents on the forehead
Formed in the air.

This is a dead scene forever now.
Nothing will ever stir.
The end will never brighten it more than this,
Nor the rain blur.

The water will always fall, and will not fall,
And the tipped bell make no sound.
The grass will always be growing for hay
Deep on the ground.

And I shall stand here like a shadow
Under the great balanced day,
My eyes on the yellow dust, that was lifting in the wind,
And does not drift away.

Women

Women have no wilderness in them,
They are provident instead,
Content in the tight hot cell of their hearts
To eat dusty bread.

They do not see cattle cropping red winter grass,
They do not hear
Snow water going down under culverts
Shallow and clear.

They wait, when they should turn to journeys,
They stiffen, when they should bend.
They use against themselves that benevolence
To which no man is friend.

They cannot think of so many crops to a field
Or of clean wood cleft by an axe.
Their love is an eager meaninglessness
Too tense, or too lax.

They hear in every whisper that speaks to them
A shout and a cry.
As like as not, when they take life over their door-sills
They should let it go by.

GWENDOLYN BROOKS (1917–   )

Gwendolyn Brooks wrote many poems as a child in Chicago and published in *American Childhood* when she was thirteen. She won several poetry competitions during the next few years and her first book, *A Street in Bronzeville*, was praised by critics. *Annie Allen* (1949) earned Brooks the Pulitzer Prize in 1950, making her the first black to receive this honor in any category. Her other works include a novel, *Maud Martha* (1953), *The Bean Eaters* (1960), *In the Mecca* (1968), two autobiographies, and children's books. In addition, several of her poems have been published in *The Hyde Parker*, a community newspaper in Chicago. Brooks has taught poetry at local colleges in Chicago and, in 1968, was named poet laureate of Illinois, succeeding Carl Sandburg.

Jessie Mitchell's Mother

Into her mother's bedroom to wash the ballooning body.
"My mother is jelly-hearted and she has a brain of jelly:
Sweet, quiver-soft, irrelevant. Not essential.
Only a habit would cry if she should die.
A pleasant sort of fool without the least iron. . . .
Are you better, mother, do you think it will come today?"
The stretched yellow rag that was Jessie Mitchell's mother
Reviewed her. Young, and so thin, and so straight.
So straight! as if nothing could ever bend her.
But poor men would bend her, and doing things with poor men,
Being much in bed, and babies would bend her over,
And the rest of things in life that were for poor women,
Coming to them grinning and pretty with intent to bend and to kill.
Comparisons shattered her heart, ate at her bulwarks:
The shabby and the bright: she, almost hating her daughter,
Crept into an old sly refuge: "Jessie's black
And her way will be black, and jerkier even than mine.
Mine, in fact, because I was lovely, had flowers
Tucked in the jerks, flowers were here and there. . . ."
She revived for the moment settled and dried-up triumphs,
Forced perfume into old petals, pulled up the droop,
Refueled
Triumphant long-exhaled breaths.
Her exquisite yellow youth. . . .

217

SYLVIA PLATH (1932–1963)

Sylvia Plath sold her first poem to *Seventeen* magazine when she was still in high school in Massachusetts. She entered Smith College in 1951 and was co-winner of the *Mademoiselle* magazine fiction contest in 1952. While in college, Plath suffered a deep depression and breakdown, and was hospitalized for a time. She married English poet Ted Hughes in 1956 and attended Newnham College, Cambridge, on a Fulbright scholarship. In 1960, her first poetry book, *The Colossus*, appeared. Under the pseudonym "Victoria Lucas," Plath published a semi-autobiographical novel, *The Bell Jar*, in 1963. Her powerful poems were famous for their anxiety, hostility, and self-revelation. Plath committed suicide on February 11, 1963, at the age of thirty-one. Her last poems were collected in *Ariel* (1965) and in several other editions in the 1970s.

Daddy

You do not do, you do not do
Any more, black shoe
In which I have lived like a foot
For thirty years, poor and white,
Barely daring to breathe or Achoo.

Daddy, I have had to kill you.
You died before I had time—
Marble-heavy, a bag full of God,
Ghastly statue with one gray toe
Big as a Frisco seal

And a head in the freakish Atlantic
Where it pours bean green over blue
In the waters off beautiful Nauset.
I used to pray to recover you.
Ach, du.

In the German tongue, in the Polish town
Scraped flat by the roller
Of wars, wars, wars.
But the name of the town is common.
My Polack friend

Says there are a dozen or two.
So I never could tell where you
Put your foot, your root,

I never could talk to you.
The tongue stuck in my jaw.

It stuck in a barb wire snare.
Ich, ich, ich, ich,
I could hardly speak.
I thought every German was you.
And the language obscene

An engine, an engine
Chuffing me off like a Jew.
A Jew to Dachau, Auschwitz, Belsen.
I began to talk like a Jew.
I think I may well be a Jew.

The snows of the Tyrol, the clear beer of Vienna
Are not very pure or true.
With my gipsy ancestress and my weird luck
And my Taroc pack and my Taroc pack
I may be a bit of a Jew.

I have always been scared of *you*,
With your Luftwaffe, your gobbledygoo.
And your neat mustache
And your Aryan eye, bright blue.
Panzer-man, panzer-man, O You—

Not God but a swastika
So black no sky could squeak through.
Every woman adores a Fascist,
The boot in the face, the brute
Brute heart of a brute like you.

You stand at the blackboard, daddy,
In the picture I have of you,
A cleft in your chin instead of your foot
But no less a devil for that, no not
Any less the black man who

Bit my pretty red heart in two.
I was ten when they buried you.
At twenty I tried to die
And get back, back, back to you.
I thought even the bones would do.

But they pulled me out of the sack,
And they stuck me together with glue.
And then I knew what to do.
I made a model of you,
A man in black with a Meinkampf look

And a love of the rack and the screw.
And I said I do, I do.
So daddy, I'm finally through.
The black telephone's off at the root,
The voices just can't worm through.

If I've killed one man, I've killed two—
The vampire who said he was you
And drank my blood for a year,
Seven years, if you want to know.
Daddy, you can lie back now.

There's a stake in your fat black heart
And the villagers never liked you.
They are dancing and stamping on you.
They always *knew* it was you.
Daddy, daddy, you bastard, I'm through.

Lady Lazarus

I have done it again.
One year in every ten
I manage it—

A sort of walking miracle, my skin
Bright as a Nazi lampshade,
My right foot

A paperweight,
My face a featureless, fine
Jew linen.

Peel off the napkin
O my enemy.
Do I terrify?—

The nose, the eye pits, the full set of teeth?
The sour breath
Will vanish in a day.

Soon, soon the flesh
The grave cave ate will be
At home on me

And I a smiling woman.
I am only thirty.
And like the cat I have nine times to die.

This is Number Three.
What a trash
To annihilate each decade.

What a million filaments.
The peanut-crunching crowd
Shoves in to see

Them unwrap me hand and foot—
The big strip tease.
Gentleman, ladies,

These are my hands,
My knees.
I may be skin and bone,

Nevertheless, I am the same, identical woman.
The first time it happened I was ten.
It was an accident.

The second time I meant
To last it out and not come back at all.
I rocked shut

As a seashell.
They had to call and call
And pick the worms off me like sticky pearls.

Dying
Is an art, like everything else.
I do it exceptionally well.

I do it so it feels like hell.
I do it so it feels real.
I guess you could say I've a call.

It's easy enough to do it in a cell.
It's easy enough to do it and stay put.
It's the theatrical

Comeback in broad day
To the same place, the same face, the same brute
Amused shout:

"A miracle!"
That knocks me out.
There is a charge

For the eyeing of my scars, there is a charge
For the hearing of my heart—
It really goes.

And there is a charge, very large charge,
For a word or a touch
Or a bit of blood

Or a piece of my hair or my clothes.
So, so, Herr Doktor.
So, Herr Enemy.

I am your opus,
I am your valuable,
The pure gold baby

That melts to a shriek.
I turn and burn.
Do not think I underestimate your great concern.

Ash, ash—
You poke and stir.
Flesh, bone, there is nothing there—

A cake of soap,
A wedding ring,
A gold filling.

Herr God, Herr Lucifer,
Beware
Beware.

Out of the ash
I rise with my red hair
And I eat men like air.

Alphabetical List of Poets

Alphabetical List of Titles and First Lines

Titles are given, in italics, only when distinct from the first lines.

225

DOVER · THRIFT · EDITIONS

All books complete and unabridged. All 5³⁄₁₆ x 8¹⁄₄, paperbound.
Just $1.00—$2.00 in U.S.A.

A selection of the more than 200 titles in the series.

POETRY

DOVER BEACH AND OTHER POEMS, Matthew Arnold. 112pp. 28037-3 $1.00

BHAGAVADGITA, Bhagavadgita. 112pp. 27782-8 $1.00

SONGS OF INNOCENCE AND SONGS OF EXPERIENCE, William Blake. 64pp. 27051-3 $1.00

THE CLASSIC TRADITION OF HAIKU: An Anthology, Faubion Bowers (ed.). 96pp. 29274-6 $1.50

SONNETS FROM THE PORTUGUESE AND OTHER POEMS, Elizabeth Barrett Browning. 64pp. 27052-1 $1.00

MY LAST DUCHESS AND OTHER POEMS, Robert Browning. 128pp. 27783-6 $1.00

POEMS AND SONGS, Robert Burns. 96pp. 26863-2 $1.00

SELECTED POEMS, George Gordon, Lord Byron. 112pp. 27784-4 $1.00

THE RIME OF THE ANCIENT MARINER AND OTHER POEMS, Samuel Taylor Coleridge. 80pp. 27266-4 $1.00

SELECTED POEMS, Emily Dickinson. 64pp. 26466-1 $1.00

SELECTED POEMS, John Donne. 96pp. 27788-7 $1.00

THE RUBÁIYÁT OF OMAR KHAYYÁM: FIRST AND FIFTH EDITIONS, Edward FitzGerald. 64pp. 26467-X $1.00

A BOY'S WILL AND NORTH OF BOSTON, Robert Frost. 112pp. (Available in U.S. only) 26866-7 $1.00

THE ROAD NOT TAKEN AND OTHER POEMS, Robert Frost. 64pp. (Available in U.S. only) 27550-7 $1.00

A SHROPSHIRE LAD, A. E. Housman. 64pp. 26468-8 $1.00

LYRIC POEMS, John Keats. 80pp. 26871-3 $1.00

THE BOOK OF PSALMS, King James Bible. 128pp. 27541-8 $1.00

GUNGA DIN AND OTHER FAVORITE POEMS, Rudyard Kipling. 80pp. 26471-8 $1.00

THE CONGO AND OTHER POEMS, Vachel Lindsay. 96pp. 27272-9 $1.00

FAVORITE POEMS, Henry Wadsworth Longfellow. 96pp. 27273-7 $1.00

SPOON RIVER ANTHOLOGY, Edgar Lee Masters. 144pp. 27275-3 $1.00

RENASCENCE AND OTHER POEMS, Edna St. Vincent Millay. 64pp. (Available in U.S. only) 26873-X $1.00

SELECTED POEMS, John Milton. 128pp. 27554-X $1.00

GREAT SONNETS, Paul Negri (ed.). 96pp. 28052-7 $1.00

THE RAVEN AND OTHER FAVORITE POEMS, Edgar Allan Poe. 64pp. 26685-0 $1.00

ESSAY ON MAN AND OTHER POEMS, Alexander Pope. 128pp. 28053-5 $1.00

GOBLIN MARKET AND OTHER POEMS, Christina Rossetti. 64pp. 28055-1 $1.00

CHICAGO POEMS, Carl Sandburg. 80pp. 28057-8 $1.00

THE SHOOTING OF DAN MCGREW AND OTHER POEMS, Robert Service. 96pp. 27556-6 $1.00

COMPLETE SONGS FROM THE PLAYS, William Shakespeare. 80pp. 27801-8 $1.00

COMPLETE SONNETS, William Shakespeare. 80pp. 26686-9 $1.00

SELECTED POEMS, Percy Bysshe Shelley. 128pp. 27558-2 $1.00

100 BEST-LOVED POEMS, Philip Smith (ed.). 96pp. 28553-7 $1.00

NATIVE AMERICAN SONGS AND POEMS: An Anthology, Brian Swann (ed.). 64pp. 29450-1 $1.00

SELECTED POEMS, Alfred Lord Tennyson. 112pp. 27282-6 $1.00

CHRISTMAS CAROLS: COMPLETE VERSES, Shane Weller (ed.). 64pp. 27397-0 $1.00

DOVER · THRIFT · EDITIONS

All books complete and unabridged. All 5³⁄₁₆ x 8¹⁄₄, paperbound.
Just $1.00—$2.00 in U.S.A.

GREAT LOVE POEMS, Shane Weller (ed.). 128pp. 27284-2 $1.00
SELECTED POEMS, Walt Whitman. 128pp. 26878-0 $1.00
THE BALLAD OF READING GAOL AND OTHER POEMS, Oscar Wilde. 64pp. 27072-6 $1.00
FAVORITE POEMS, William Wordsworth. 80pp. 27073-4 $1.00
EARLY POEMS, William Butler Yeats. 128pp. 27808-5 $1.00

FICTION

FLATLAND: A ROMANCE OF MANY DIMENSIONS, Edwin A. Abbott. 96pp. 27263-X $1.00
PERSUASION, Jane Austen. 224pp. 29555-9 $2.00
PRIDE AND PREJUDICE, Jane Austen. 272pp. 28473-5 $2.00
SENSE AND SENSIBILITY, Jane Austen. 272pp. 29049-2 $2.00
BEOWULF, Beowulf (trans. by R. K. Gordon). 64pp. 27264-8 $1.00
CIVIL WAR STORIES, Ambrose Bierce. 128pp. 28038-1 $1.00
TARZAN OF THE APES, Edgar Rice Burroughs. 224pp. 29570-2 $2.00
ALICE'S ADVENTURES IN WONDERLAND, Lewis Carroll. 96pp. 27543-4 $1.00
O PIONEERS!, Willa Cather. 128pp. 27785-2 $1.00
FIVE GREAT SHORT STORIES, Anton Chekhov. 96pp. 26463-7 $1.00
FAVORITE FATHER BROWN STORIES, G. K. Chesterton. 96pp. 27545-0 $1.00
THE AWAKENING, Kate Chopin. 128pp. 27786-0 $1.00
HEART OF DARKNESS, Joseph Conrad. 80pp. 26464-5 $1.00
THE SECRET SHARER AND OTHER STORIES, Joseph Conrad. 128pp. 27546-9 $1.00
THE "LITTLE REGIMENT" AND OTHER CIVIL WAR STORIES, Stephen Crane. 80pp. 29557-5 $1.00
THE OPEN BOAT AND OTHER STORIES, Stephen Crane. 128pp. 27547-7 $1.00
THE RED BADGE OF COURAGE, Stephen Crane. 112pp. 26465-3 $1.00
A CHRISTMAS CAROL, Charles Dickens. 80pp. 26865-9 $1.00
THE CRICKET ON THE HEARTH AND OTHER CHRISTMAS STORIES, Charles Dickens. 128pp. 28039-X $1.00
THE DOUBLE, Fyodor Dostoyevsky. 128pp. 29572-9 $1.50
NOTES FROM THE UNDERGROUND, Fyodor Dostoyevsky. 96pp. 27053-X $1.00
THE ADVENTURE OF THE DANCING MEN AND OTHER STORIES, Sir Arthur Conan Doyle. 80pp. 29558-3 $1.00
SIX GREAT SHERLOCK HOLMES STORIES, Sir Arthur Conan Doyle. 112pp. 27055-6 $1.00
SILAS MARNER, George Eliot. 160pp. 29246-0 $1.50
MADAME BOVARY, Gustave Flaubert. 256pp. 29257-6 $2.00
WHERE ANGELS FEAR TO TREAD, E. M. Forster. 128pp. (Available in U.S. only) 27791-7 $1.00
THE OVERCOAT AND OTHER STORIES, Nikolai Gogol. 112pp. 27057-2 $1.00
GREAT GHOST STORIES, John Grafton (ed.). 112pp. 27270-2 $1.00
THE MABINOGION, Lady Charlotte E. Guest. 192pp. 29541-9 $2.00
THE LUCK OF ROARING CAMP AND OTHER STORIES, Bret Harte. 96pp. 27271-0 $1.00
THE SCARLET LETTER, Nathaniel Hawthorne. 192pp. 28048-9 $2.00
YOUNG GOODMAN BROWN AND OTHER STORIES, Nathaniel Hawthorne. 128pp. 27060-2 $1.00
THE GIFT OF THE MAGI AND OTHER SHORT STORIES, O. Henry. 96pp. 27061-0 $1.00
THE NUTCRACKER AND THE GOLDEN POT, E. T. A. Hoffmann. 128pp. 27806-9 $1.00
THE BEAST IN THE JUNGLE AND OTHER STORIES, Henry James. 128pp. 27552-3 $1.00
THE TURN OF THE SCREW, Henry James. 96pp. 26684-2 $1.00

DOVER · THRIFT · EDITIONS

All books complete and unabridged. All 5³⁄₁₆ x 8¼, paperbound.
Just $1.00—$2.00 in U.S.A.

DUBLINERS, James Joyce. 160pp. 26870-5 $1.00

A PORTRAIT OF THE ARTIST AS A YOUNG MAN, James Joyce. 192pp. 28050-0 $2.00

THE MAN WHO WOULD BE KING AND OTHER STORIES, Rudyard Kipling. 128pp. 28051-9 $1.00

SELECTED SHORT STORIES, D. H. Lawrence. 128pp. 27794-1 $1.00

GREEN TEA AND OTHER GHOST STORIES, J. Sheridan LeFanu. 96pp. 27795-X $1.00

THE CALL OF THE WILD, Jack London. 64pp. 26472-6 $1.00

FIVE GREAT SHORT STORIES, Jack London. 96pp. 27063-7 $1.00

WHITE FANG, Jack London. 160pp. 26968-X $1.00

THE NECKLACE AND OTHER SHORT STORIES, Guy de Maupassant. 128pp. 27064-5 $1.00

BARTLEBY AND BENITO CERENO, Herman Melville. 112pp. 26473-4 $1.00

THE GOLD-BUG AND OTHER TALES, Edgar Allan Poe. 128pp. 26875-6 $1.00

TALES OF TERROR AND DETECTION, Edgar Allan Poe. 96pp. 28744-0 $1.00

THE QUEEN OF SPADES AND OTHER STORIES, Alexander Pushkin. 128pp. 28054-3 $1.00

FRANKENSTEIN, Mary Shelley. 176pp. 28211-2 $1.00

THREE LIVES, Gertrude Stein. 176pp. 28059-4 $2.00

THE STRANGE CASE OF DR. JEKYLL AND MR. HYDE, Robert Louis Stevenson. 64pp. 26688-5 $1.00

TREASURE ISLAND, Robert Louis Stevenson. 160pp. 27559-0 $1.00

GULLIVER'S TRAVELS, Jonathan Swift. 240pp. 29273-8 $2.00

THE KREUTZER SONATA AND OTHER SHORT STORIES, Leo Tolstoy. 144pp. 27805-0 $1.00

ADVENTURES OF HUCKLEBERRY FINN, Mark Twain. 224pp. 28061-6 $2.00

THE MYSTERIOUS STRANGER AND OTHER STORIES, Mark Twain. 128pp. 27069-6 $1.00

CANDIDE, Voltaire (François-Marie Arouet). 112pp. 26689-3 $1.00

"THE COUNTRY OF THE BLIND" AND OTHER SCIENCE-FICTION STORIES, H. G. Wells. 160pp. (Available in U.S. only) 29569-9 $1.50

THE INVISIBLE MAN, H. G. Wells. 112pp. (Available in U.S. only) 27071-8 $1.00

THE WAR OF THE WORLDS, H. G. Wells. 160pp. (Available in U.S. only) 29506-0 $1.00

ETHAN FROME, Edith Wharton. 96pp. 26690-7 $1.00

THE PICTURE OF DORIAN GRAY, Oscar Wilde. 192pp. 27807-7 $1.00

MONDAY OR TUESDAY: Eight Stories, Virginia Woolf. 64pp. 29453-6 $1.00

NONFICTION

THE DEVIL'S DICTIONARY, Ambrose Bierce. 144pp. 27542-6 $1.00

THE SOULS OF BLACK FOLK, W. E. B. Du Bois. 176pp. 28041-1 $2.00

SELF-RELIANCE AND OTHER ESSAYS, Ralph Waldo Emerson. 128pp. 27790-9 $1.00

THE AUTOBIOGRAPHY OF BENJAMIN FRANKLIN, Benjamin Franklin. 144pp. 29073-5 $1.50

THE STORY OF MY LIFE, Helen Keller. 80pp. 29249-5 $1.00

GREAT SPEECHES, Abraham Lincoln. 112pp. 26872-1 $1.00

THE PRINCE, Niccolò Machiavelli. 80pp. 27274-5 $1.00

SYMPOSIUM AND PHAEDRUS, Plato. 96pp. 27798-4 $1.00

THE TRIAL AND DEATH OF SOCRATES: Four Dialogues, Plato. 128pp. 27066-1 $1.00

CIVIL DISOBEDIENCE AND OTHER ESSAYS, Henry David Thoreau. 96pp. 27563-9 $1.00

THE THEORY OF THE LEISURE CLASS, Thorstein Veblen. 256pp. 28062-4 $2.00

DOVER · THRIFT · EDITIONS

All books complete and unabridged. All 5³⁄₁₆ x 8¼, paperbound.
Just $1.00—$2.00 in U.S.A.

PLAYS

PROMETHEUS BOUND, Aeschylus. 64pp. 28762-9 $1.00

WHAT EVERY WOMAN KNOWS, James Barrie. 80pp. 29578-8 $1.50

THE CHERRY ORCHARD, Anton Chekhov. 64pp. 26682-6 $1.00

THE THREE SISTERS, Anton Chekhov. 64pp. 27544-2 $1.00

THE WAY OF THE WORLD, William Congreve. 80pp. 27787-9 $1.00

BACCHAE, Euripides. 64pp. 29580-X $1.00

MEDEA, Euripides. 64pp. 27548-5 $1.00

THE MIKADO, William Schwenck Gilbert. 64pp. 27268-0 $1.00

FAUST, PART ONE, Johann Wolfgang von Goethe. 192pp. 28046-2 $2.00

SHE STOOPS TO CONQUER, Oliver Goldsmith. 80pp. 26867-5 $1.00

A DOLL'S HOUSE, Henrik Ibsen. 80pp. 27062-9 $1.00

HEDDA GABLER, Henrik Ibsen. 80pp. 26469-6 $1.00

VOLPONE, Ben Jonson. 112pp. 28049-7 $1.00

DR. FAUSTUS, Christopher Marlowe. 64pp. 28208-2 $1.00

THE MISANTHROPE, Molière. 64pp. 27065-3 $1.00

THE EMPEROR JONES, Eugene O'Neill. 64pp. 29268-1 $1.50

RIGHT YOU ARE, IF YOU THINK YOU ARE, Luigi Pirandello. 64pp. 29576-1 $1.50

HANDS AROUND, Arthur Schnitzler. 64pp. 28724-6 $1.00

HAMLET, William Shakespeare. 128pp. 27278-8 $1.00

HENRY IV, William Shakespeare. 96pp. 29584-2 $1.00

JULIUS CAESAR, William Shakespeare. 80pp. 26876-4 $1.00

KING LEAR, William Shakespeare. 112pp. 28058-6 $1.00

MACBETH, William Shakespeare. 96pp. 27802-6 $1.00

A MIDSUMMER NIGHT'S DREAM, William Shakespeare. 80pp. 27067-X $1.00

ROMEO AND JULIET, William Shakespeare. 96pp. 27557-4 $1.00

ARMS AND THE MAN, George Bernard Shaw. 80pp. (Available in U.S. only) 26476-9 $1.00

THE SCHOOL FOR SCANDAL, Richard Brinsley Sheridan. 96pp. 26687-7 $1.00

ANTIGONE, Sophocles. 64pp. 27804-2 $1.00

OEDIPUS REX, Sophocles. 64pp. 26877-2 $1.00

MISS JULIE, August Strindberg. 64pp. 27281-8 $1.00

THE PLAYBOY OF THE WESTERN WORLD AND RIDERS TO THE SEA, J. M. Synge. 80pp. 27562-0 $1.00

THE IMPORTANCE OF BEING EARNEST, Oscar Wilde. 64pp. 26478-5 $1.00

For a complete descriptive list of all volumes in the Dover Thrift Editions series
write for a free Dover Fiction and Literature Catalog (59047-X) to
Dover Publications, Inc., Dept. DTE, 31 E. 2nd Street, Mineola, N.Y. 11501